Medicinal and Aromatic Plants

NIPA® GENX ELECTRONIC RESOURCES & SOLUTIONS P. LTD.
New Delhi-110 034

About the Authors

Dr. Sindhu P. V. is an Assistant Professor of Agronomy at AICRP on Medicinal and Aromatic Plants, Kerala Agricultural University, Thrissur, Kerala, India. She holds a Ph.D. in Agronomy from Kerala Agricultural University. With over 20 years of experience in teaching and research, Dr. Sindhu specializes in Agronomy, focusing on medicinal and aromatic plants. She has handled several research projects and published extensively in peer-reviewed journals and books. Her major research contributions include developing good agricultural practices for medicinal and aromatic plants and standardizing semi-processing methods to promote cultivation among small and marginal farmers.

Dr Pradeepkumar T. took PhD in Horticulture from IARI New Delhi and undergone overseas training at University of Wisconsin, USA. He is holding the charge of Vice Chancellor, Kerala University of Fisheries and Ocean Studies, Kochin, Kerala and working as Professor and Head, Department of Vegetable Science, Kerala Agricultural University. Dr Pradeepkumar.T has experience of more than 30 years in horticultural research, teaching and extension as state and national level expert. He has developed 8 hybrids of different crops like water melon (Seedless types), salad cucumber (Parthenocarpic type), bitter gourd and ridge gourd. He was the editor of Journal of Tropical Agriculture for six years and reviewer of springer and elseiver publications. He is the recipient of Krishi Vijnan Award for the best agricultural scientist instituted by Govt. of Kerala and Harbhajan Singh Award by ISVS. He has published 92 research papers, 12 books, 18 book chapters and 45 popular article. He received ISVS fellowship from, Indian Society of Vegetable Science in year 2016, IAHS fellowship from Indian Academy of Horticultural Science in the year 2019 and ISS fellowship from Indian Society for Spices in the year 2021.

Medicinal and Aromatic Plants

Sindhu P. V.
Assistant Professor of Agronomy
at AICRP on Medicinal and Aromatic Plants
Kerala Agricultural University, Thrissur, Kerala, India

Pradeepkumar T.
Professor and Head
Department of Vegetable Science
Kerala Agricultural University
Thrissur, Kerala, India

NIPA® GENX ELECTRONIC RESOURCES & SOLUTIONS P. LTD.
New Delhi-110 034

NIPA® GENX ELECTRONIC
RESOURCES & SOLUTIONS P. LTD.
101,103, Vikas Surya Plaza, CU Block
L.S.C. Market, Pitam Pura, New Delhi-110 034
Ph : +91-11-43860225, Mob.: +91 9717133558, 9540816132
E-mail: newindiapublishingagency@gmail.com
Website: www.nipaersources.com

Print ISBN: 978-93-58879-49-0
ebook ISBN: 978-93-58875-77-5

Composed and Designed by NIPA®.

Preface

For centuries, medicinal and aromatic plants have played a vital role in human health, wellness, and culture. From ancient civilizations to modern times, these plants have been revered for their therapeutic properties, fragrance, and flavor. The use of medicinal and aromatic plants has transcended geographical boundaries, with various cultures developing their unique traditions and practices.

This comprehensive book aims to explore the fascinating world of **medicinal and aromatic plants,** exploring their history, diversity, significance, and value addition. Various topics, from the basics of medicinal and aromatic plants to advanced concepts were included, making it a valuable resource for students, researchers, farmers, and enthusiasts.

The book is divided into several sections, each focusing on a specific aspect of medicinal and aromatic plants. Descriptions of various medicinal and aromatic plants, their botanical characteristics, medicinal properties, and uses were explained in detail. The book also discussed good agricultural practices, harvesting techniques, and post-harvest management strategies to ensure the quality and sustainability of these plants.

In addition, various aspects of value addition is explored in medicinal and aromatic plants, including processing and product development. To facilitate better understanding, each chapter includes frequently asked questions and their answers.

Our goal is to provide a comprehensive and authoritative resource that will meet the needs of various stakeholders, including students, farmers, researchers, entrepreneurs, and policymakers. We hope that this book will inspire and inform readers and contribute to the sustainable development of the medicinal and aromatic plants sector.

Authors

Contents

1

Medicinal and Aromatic Plants in India: Cultivation, Opportunities and Challenges

Introduction

India, renowned for its rich biodiversity and ancient tradition of Ayurveda, is home to an astonishing array of medicinal and aromatic plants. These plants, harboring bioactive compounds such as alkaloids, glycosides, terpenes, and flavonoids, have been harnessed for centuries to prevent, diagnose, and treat various health ailments. Medicinal plants, utilizing parts like leaves, roots, stems, or seeds, offer natural remedies for wellness. Meanwhile, aromatic plants, rich in fragrant volatile oils, are the cornerstone of essential oils, aromatherapy, and perfumery.

A Legacy of Healing: History of Medicinal and Aromatic Plant Cultivation in India

Ancient India (3000 BCE - 500 CE)

Ayurveda's origins: Ayurveda, the traditional Indian system of medicine, emerged around 3000 BCE, emphasizing the use of medicinal plants.

Vedic period (1500 BCE - 500 BCE)

- Ayurvedic texts like the Rigveda, Yajurveda, and Atharvaveda documented medicinal plant uses.
- Charaka Samhita and Sushruta Samhita (400 BCE - 200 CE): These seminal texts systematically described medicinal plant properties and uses.
- Trade and cultural exchange: India's strategic location on the Silk Road facilitated trade with China, the Middle East, and the Mediterranean.

Medieval period (500 - 1500 CE)

- Unani medicine introduction (8th century CE): Arab traders brought Unani medicine, increasing demand for medicinal plants.

- Islamic influence (12th - 16th century CE): Unani medicine merged with Ayurveda, enriching India's medicinal plant heritage.
- Delhi Sultanate and Mughal Empire (13th - 19th century CE): Royal patronage supported medicinal plant cultivation and trade.

British Colonial Era (1500 - 1947 CE)

British East India Company (17th - 19th century CE): Exploitation of India's medicinal plant resources led to:

- Over-exploitation of wild resources.
- Decline of traditional cultivation practices.
- Export of medicinal plants to Britain.
- Colonization and forced cultivation (19th century CE): British established plantations for commercial crops like indigo, tea, and cinchona.

Post-Independence (1947 - 1980 CE)

- Modern medicine emphasis (1947 - 1960s CE): India focused on modern medicine, neglecting traditional practices.
- Decline of medicinal plant cultivation (1960s - 1980s CE): Lack of government support and research led to decline.

Revival and growth (1980s - 1990s CE)

- Government initiatives (1980s CE): National Medicinal Plants Board (NMPb)established to promote cultivation.
- Institutional support (1990s CE): Research institutions like the Central Institute of Medicinal and Aromatic Plants (CIMAP) emerged.

Modern era (2000s CE - present)

- Organic and sustainable practices: Increased focus on environmentally friendly cultivation.
- Export-oriented production: India became a significant exporter of medicinal and aromatic plants.
- Research and development: Newproducts, technologies, and formulations emerged.
- Growing demand: Herbal medicines, aromatherapy, and natural products gained popularity.

Key milestones

- 1980: National Medicinal Plants Board (NMPB) established.
- 1985: Central Institute of Medicinal and Aromatic Plants (CIMAP) founded.

- 2000: India's first medicinal plant export zone established.
- 2010: National Ayush Mission launched to promote traditional medicine.

Scope and importance of medicinal plant cultivation in India

Medicinal plant cultivation holds immense significance in India, offering a plethora of economic, social, and environmental benefits. With its rich biodiversity and ancient tradition of Ayurveda, India is home to over 8,000 medicinal plant species, accounting for 70% of the world's total. This chapter delves into the scope and importance of medicinal plant cultivation in India, highlighting its potential for growth, challenges, and future directions.

The economic importance of medicinal plant cultivation in India cannot be overstated. The industry generates substantial employment opportunities, supporting rural livelihoods and employing over 1 million people. Furthermore, India's medicinal plant industry has a significant export revenue, valued at INR150 billion in 2020, with a domestic market worth INR 400 billion. This contributes significantly to rural development, enhancing infrastructure and the economy.

Beyond economic benefits, medicinal plant cultivation holds profound social importance. It provides affordable, traditional medicine to millions, safeguarding cultural heritage and empowering rural communities through self-sufficiency. The preservation of traditional knowledge and Ayurvedic heritage is crucial, ensuring the continued availability of natural remedies.

Environmentally, medicinal plant cultivation promotes sustainable agriculture practices, conserving biodiversity and protecting endangered species. Organic farming methods maintain soil health and fertility, contributing to eco-friendly agriculture.

The scope for growth in India's medicinal plant cultivation is substantial. Increasing global demand for herbal medicines, government initiatives such as the National Ayush Mission and National Medicinal Plants Board, and research-driven product development present opportunities for expansion. International collaborations and export-oriented production further enhance the industry's potential.

However, challenges persist, including sustainable cultivation practices, quality control, regulatory frameworks, and market access. Addressing these concerns is crucial for the industry's continued growth.

In conclusion, medicinal plant cultivation in India offers vast potential for economic, social, and environmental benefits. With targeted initiatives and sustainable practices, India can solidify its position as a global leader in the medicinal plant industry.

Area under medicinal plant cultivation in India

According to the National Medicinal Plants Board, the area under medicinal plant cultivation in India is increasing steadily. Here are some approximate figures:

- 2019-2020: 15,000 hectares (37,065 acres)
- 2020-2021: 20,000 hectares (49,421 acres)
- 2021-2022: 25,000 hectares (61,776 acres)

Top medicinal plant-cultivating States

1. Uttarakhand: 5,000 hectares (12,355 acres)
2. Himachal Pradesh: 3,000 hectares (7,413 acres)
3. Jammu and Kashmir: 2,500 hectares (6,178 acres)
4. Kerala: 2,000 hectares (4,942 acres)
5. Tamil Nadu: 1,500 hectares (3,707 acres)

Constraints in medicinal plant cultivation

1. Climate and soil specificity: Many medicinal plants require specific climate and soil conditions, limiting cultivation areas.
2. Seed qvailability and quality: Limited availability of high-quality seeds for medicinal plants.
3. Water availability: Irrigation requirements for medicinal plants can strain water resources.
4. Pests and Diseases: Susceptibility to pests and diseases, affecting crop yields and quality.
5. Labor shortages: Labor-intensive cultivation and harvesting processes.
6. Lack of standardization: Variability in cultivation practices, affecting quality and consistency.
7. Regulatory framework: Complex regulatory environment, requiring compliance with multiple laws.
8. Marketing and sales: Limited market access, sales channels, and product promotion.
9. Research and development: Limited research on medicinal plant cultivation, processing, and product development.
10. Infrastructure: Inadequate infrastructure, including storage, transportation, and processing facilities.
11. Quality control: Ensuring consistent quality of medicinal plants and products.

12. Certification and accreditation: Obtaining certifications (e.g., GMP, ISO) and accredit
13. Competition: Competition from other countries, synthetic products, and adulterated products.
14. Policy support: Limited policy support, incentives, and subsidies.
15. Environmental concerns: Sustainable cultivation practices, conservation, and environmental impact.
16. Intellectual property: Protection of indigenous knowledge, patents, and trademarks.
17. Supply chain management: Managing supply chains, from cultivation to end-products.
18. Farmers' training: Educating farmers on best practices, new technologies, and market trends.

By addressing these challenges and leveraging opportunities, India can strengthen its position as a global leader in medicinal plant cultivation and promote a thriving herbal industry.

MCQ questions

1. When did Ayurveda, the traditional Indian system of medicine, emerge?

   a) 1500 BCE b) 3000 BCE

   c) 500 CE d) 1000 CE

2. Which of the following texts systematically described medicinal plant properties and uses?

   a) Rigveda

   b) Charaka Samhita and Sushruta Samhita

   c) Yajurveda

   d) Atharvaveda

3. What is the estimated value of India's medicinal plant industry in 2020?

   a) ₹ 100 billion b) ₹ 150 billion

   c) ₹ 200 billion d) ₹ 250 billion

4. According to the National Medicinal Plants Board, what is the approximate area under medicinal plant cultivation in India in 2021-2022?

   a) 10,000 hectares b) 15,000 hectares

   c) 20,000 hectares d) 25,000 hectares

5. Which state in India has the largest area under medicinal plant cultivation?

   a) Uttarakhand b) Himachal Pradesh

   c) Jammu and Kashmir d) Kerala

6. What is one of the major constraints in medicinal plant cultivation in India?

   a) Climate and soil specificity b) Seed availability and quality

   c) Water availability d) All of the above

7. What is the name of the mission launched by the Indian government in 2010 to promote traditional medicine?

   a) National Ayush Mission

   b) National Medicinal Plants Board

   c) Central Institute of Medicinal and Aromatic Plants

   d) None of the above

8. Which of the following is a challenge faced by the medicinal plant industry in India?

   a) Limited market access b) Lack of standardization

   c) Regulatory framework d) All of the above

9. What is the estimated number of people employed in the medicinal plant industry in India?

   a) 500,000 b) 1 million

   c) 1.5 million d) 2 million

10. What is one of the environmental benefits of medicinal plant cultivation in India?

    a) Conservation of biodiversity

    b) Protection of endangered species

    c) Promotion of sustainable agriculture practices

    d) All of the above

Short answer questions

1. What are the economic benefits of medicinal plant cultivation in India?
2. Describe the significance of Ayurveda in the context of medicinal plant cultivation in India.
3. What are some of the challenges faced by farmers in medicinal plant cultivation in India?

4. How does medicinal plant cultivation contribute to environmental sustainability in India?
5. What initiatives has the Indian government taken to promote medicinal plant cultivation and the herbal industry?

Answers for MCQ

1. b) 3000 BCE
2. b) Charaka Samhita and Sushruta Samhita
3. b) ₹ 150 billion
4. d) 25,000 hectares
5. a) Uttarakhand
6. d) All of the above (climate and soil specificity, seed availability and quality, water availability)
7. a) National Ayush Mission
8. d) All of the above (limited market access, lack of standardization, regulatory framework)
9. b) 1 million
10. d) All of the above (conservation of biodiversity, protection of endangered species, promotion of sustainable agriculture practices)

References

Chatterjee, S.K., 2001, July. Cultivation of medicinal and aromatic plants in India-A commercial approach. In International Conference on Medicinal and Aromatic Plants. Possibilities and Limitations of Medicinal and Aromatic Plant 576 (pp. 191-202).

Gowthami, R., Sharma, N., Pandey, R. and Agrawal, A., 2021. Status and consolidated list of threatened medicinal plants of India. Genetic Resources and Crop Evolution, 68(6), pp.2235-2263.

Kala, C.P., 2015. Medicinal and aromatic plants: Boon for enterprise development. Journal of Applied Research on Medicinal and Aromatic Plants, 2(4), pp.134-139.

Mahajon, B., Dwivedi, H., Vijayakumar, V., Sanwal, C.S. and Nesari, T.M., 2023. Research and development activities under central sector scheme of the National Medicinal Plants Board, India. Medicinal Plants-International Journal of Phytomedicines and Related Industries, 15(3), pp.610-618.

Parveen, B., Parveen, A., Parveen, R., Ahmad, S., Ahmad, M. and Iqbal, M., 2020. Challenges and opportunities for traditional herbal medicine today, with special reference to its status in India. Ann Phytomed, 9(2), pp.97-112.

2

Betel Vine

Scientific name: *Piper betle L.*

Family: Piperaceae

The betel vine, scientifically known as *Piper betle* L., is a perennial climber native to Southeast Asia, including India. It belongs to the Piperaceae family. The betel vine has been an integral part of Indian culture, tradition, and medicine for thousands of years.

In Hinduism, the betel vine is considered a sacred plant, often offered to gods and goddesses. The leaves are used in various rituals, including weddings and pujas (prayer ceremonies). In Indian tradition, betel leaves are also offered as a mark of respect and hospitality to guests.

Betel leaves have been used in Ayurvedic medicine for their numerous health benefits. They are rich in antioxidants, anti-inflammatory compounds, and essential oils. The leaves are used to treat various ailments, including digestive issues, respiratory problems, skin conditions, and oral health issues.

In addition to their medicinal properties, betel leaves are also used as a mouth and breathe freshener. The leaves are chewed with betel nuts (areca nuts) and lime, a practice known as "paan" in India. The betel vine is a versatile plant with significant cultural, medicinal, and economic importance in India and other parts of Southeast Asia.

Chemical constituents

Betel vine contains a variety of bioactive compounds, including:

1. Alkaloids: Piperine, piperlongumin, pellitorine, and piperolein B.
2. Phenolic compounds: Eugenol, hydroxychavicol, and chavibetol.
3. Flavonoids: Quercetin, kaempferol, and isorhapontigenin.
4. Terpenoids: Caryophyllene, humulene, and germacrene D.
5. Glycosides: Piperine glycoside and pellitorine glycoside.
6. Volatile oils: Eugenol, beta-caryophyllene, and alpha-humulene.

These chemical constituents contribute to betel vine's medicinal and aromatic properties, making it a valuable crop for various applications.

Origin and distribution

Betel vine is native to Southeast Asia and India, with cultivation spreading to:

Tropical regions of Africa (Nigeria, Ghana), Pacific Islands (Fiji, Samoa), and Southeast Asia (Indonesia, Malaysia).

Botany

Betel Vine is a perennial, evergreen climber belonging to the family Piperaceae. It is native to Southeast Asia and the Indian subcontinent, and is commonly cultivated in many parts of Asia for its leaves. The plant has a slender, cylindrical stem with heart-shaped, alternate leaves that are 5-7 cm long and 3-5 cm wide. The inflorescence is spike-like, 5-7 cm long, bearing minute, white, and unisexual flowers. The fruits are small, berry-like, and red.

Climatic and soil

Betel vine thrives in tropical climates characterized by high humidity. This versatile crop can be cultivated in diverse environments. In regions like Kerala, betel vine is often grown as an intercrop in arecanut and coconut plantations.

Soil-wise, betel vine prefers well-drained, fertile soils that promote healthy growth. Conversely, waterlogged, saline, and alkaline soils are not suitable for cultivation. Lateritic soils, however, have proven to be an excellent match for this crop.

To ensure successful cultivation, it is essential to provide the right conditions. These include adequate shade, irrigation, and an annual 200-450 cm annual rainfall. Betel vine can tolerate temperatures between 10°C and 40°C. However, prolonged exposure to extremely low temperatures can lead to leaf fall, while hot, dry winds can cause damage.

Varieties

Around 100 types of betel vine varieties are found worldwide. India has about 40 varieties. The main types of betel vine are Desawari, Bangla, Kapoori, Meetha, and Sanchi.

These types are grown in different parts of India. Kapoori and Sanchi are mainly grown in South India, while Bangla and Desawari are grown in North India. Meetha is only grown in West Bengal.

Major local varities under cultivation in Tamil Nadu and Kerala include Thulasi, Venmani, Arikodi, Kalkodi, Karilanchi, Karpuram, Chelanthikarpuram, Koottakkodinandan, Perumkodi, Amaravila and Pramuttan.

Season

The planting time may vary depending on the specific region, climate, and weather conditions. Generally, it is planted at the onset of southwest or northeast monsoon season. May-June and September-October, when the temperature and rainfall are adequate.

Land preparation

To cultivate betel vine, it's essential to prepare the land properly. This involves selecting a suitable location with good shade and irrigation facilities. The land is then dug thoroughly and laid out into furrows, typically 10-15 meters long, 75 cm wide, and 75 cm deep. These furrows are spaced 1 meter apart. To enrich the soil, well-rotten farm yard manure, leaves, and wood ash are thoroughly mixed into the topsoil of the furrows. A high dose of organic manure, ranging from 20-50 tons per hectare, is also applied to maintain good soil structure, which is crucial for the proper development of the root system.

Planting material and planting technique

The top portion of mature vines (2-3 years old) is used for planting betel vines. Healthy cuttings, approximately one meter long with three nodes, serve as the ideal planting material. To plant one hectare, 20,000 to 25,000 cuttings are required. Prior to planting, the furrows are irrigated. The cuttings are then planted in holes 20 cm apart in the furrows, ensuring that one node is buried in the soil and the second node is at ground level. The soil around the planted cutting is pressed firmly to encourage quick germination. Shade is provided to the planted cuttings using coconut leaves. To prevent excess moisture, hand splashing water on the vines is recommended in the early stages. Light irrigation is given four times daily until establishment in the absence of rain. The cuttings typically establish within three weeks, and the first leaf emerges in about a month.

Irrigation and drainage

Betel vine requires consistently moist soil, but excessive moisture can be detrimental. To achieve this balance, frequent light irrigations are essential. The ideal irrigation practice involves providing enough water to prevent standing water from accumulating in the bed for over half an hour. In cases of waterlogging due to heavy rainfall or excess irrigation, immediate drainage measures must be taken. For optimal results, irrigation is best done during the morning or evening when evaporation is minimal.

Trailing and weeding

After about a month, the cuttings sprout and begin to creep. At this stage, they must be trailed onto bamboo standards, erected at regular intervals, and linked together using coir rope. The vines are initially trained onto the standards using coir ties, and later, they are loosely tied to the standards at 15-20 cm intervals using banana fiber. As the vines come into contact with the standards, they develop adventitious roots, allowing them to cling to the support. Trailing is repeated every 15-20 days, depending on the growth of the vines. Regular weeding and stirring of the soil are also necessary to maintain a clean and healthy garden.

Manuring

To promote healthy growth and development, betel vine requires regular manuring. Dried leaves and wood ash are applied to the furrows at fortnightly intervals, and cowdung slurry is sprinkled over the plants. This process is repeated four months after planting until the crop is ready for harvest. Additionally, applying different types of leaves, such as gliricidia and mango leaves, at monthly intervals has been beneficial for the vines' growth.

Fertilizer application

Betel vine requires an annual application of 150 kg N/ha, 100 kg P2O5/ha, and 30 kg K/ha. The nitrogen requirement can be met by applying 75 kg N/ha through Neem cake and 75 kg N/ha through Urea. Superphosphate can be used to supply the required phosphorus, while Muriate of potash can provide the necessary potassium.

These fertilizers are applied in three split doses: the first dose 15 days after lifting the vines, and the second and third doses at 40-45 day intervals.

Harvesting

Betel vines are ready for harvesting within 3-6 months, when they reach a height of 150-180 cm and start branching. Harvesting involves removing the leaves along with their petioles using the right thumb. Once harvesting commences, it is typically continued daily or weekly. The interval between harvests varies from 15 days to a month until the next lowering of vines. It is essential to manure the vines after each harvest to promote healthy growth and maximize yields.

Yield

The average annual yield of betel leaves is approximately 75 to 100 lakh leaves per hectare.

Lowering of vines for rejuvenation

Under normal cultivation, betel vines typically grow to a height of 3 meters within a year. However, as they reach this height, their ability to produce normal-sized leaves diminishes and requires rejuvenation. This is achieved through the process of lowering the vines, which is usually done in March or April. After lowering, the tillers emerge from the nodes at the bends of the coiled vines at ground level, producing multiple primary vines. It is essential to provide irrigation after each lowering to support renewed growth.

MCQ questions

1. What is the scientific name of the betel vine?

   a) *Piper betle* L. b) *Piper longum* L.

   c) *Piper nigrum* L. d) *Piper auritum* L.

2. Which family does the betel vine belong to?

   a) Piperaceae b) Solanaceae

   c) Rutaceae d) Zingiberaceae

3. What is thc primary use of betel leaves in Ayurvedic medicine?

   a) Digestive issues b) Respiratory problems

   c) Skin conditions d) All of the above

4. How many types of betel vine varieties are found worldwide?

   a) 50 b) 100

   c) 200 d) 500

5. What is the ideal temperature range for betel vine cultivation?

   a) 10°C - 30°C b) 10°C - 40°C

   c) 20°C - 30°C d) 20°C - 40°C

6. What is the recommended annual application of nitrogen for betel vine cultivation?

   a) 100 kg N/ha b) 150 kg N/ha

   c) 200 kg N/ha d) 250 kg N/ha

7. How often should betel vines be trailed onto bamboo standards?

   a) Every 10 days b) Every 15-20 days

   c) Every 30 days d) Every 60 days

8. What is the average annual yield of betel leaves per hectare?

   a) 50-75 lakh leaves b) 75-100 lakh leaves

   c) 100-125 lakh leaves d) 125-150 lakh leaves

9. Why is it essential to lower the betel vines periodically?
   a) To promote healthy growth b) To increase yields
   c) To rejuvenate the vines d) All of the above
10. What is the recommended method for harvesting betel leaves?
   a) Removing the leaves along with their petioles using the right thumb
   b) Cutting the leaves with scissors
   c) Pulling the leaves from the stem
   d) Twisting the leaves from the stem

Short answer questions

1. Describe the cultural significance of betel vines in India.
2. What are the different types of betel vine varieties found in India?
3. Explain the process of trailing and weeding in betel vine cultivation.
4. What are the essential nutrients required for betel vine cultivation, and how are they applied?
5. Describe the process of harvesting and rejuvenating betel vines.

Answers for MCQ

1. a) *Piper betle* L.
2. a) Piperaceae
3. d) All of the above
4. b) 100
5. b) 10°C - 40°C
6. b) 150 kg N/ha
7. b) Every 15-20 days
8. b) 75-100 lakh leaves
9. d) All of the above
10. a) Removing the leaves along with their petioles using the right thumb

References

Baviskar, H.P., Dhake, G.T., Kasai, M.A., Chaudhari, N.B. and Deshmukh, T.A., 2017. Review of Piper betle. Research Journal of Pharmacognosy and Phytochemistry, 9(2), p.128.

Chibber, H.M., 1913. The morphology and histology of Piper betle, Linn.(the Betel-vine). Botanical Journal of the Linnean Society, 41(283), pp.357-383.

Mazumder, S., Roychowdhury, A. and Banerjee, S., 2016. An overview of betel leaf (Piper betle L.): A review. Ann Food Sci Technol, 17(2), pp.367-376.

Raut, S.K. and Bhattacharya, S.S., 1999. Pests and Diseases of Betelvine (Piper Betle)and Their Natural Enemies in India. Experimental & applied acarology, 23, pp.319-325.

Sengupta, K., 2019. Agronomy of Betelvine Crop. Agronomic Crops: Volume 1: Production Technologies, pp.533-543.

3

Belladona

Scientific name: *Atropa belladonna L.*

Family: Solanaceae

Belladonna, also known as deadly nightshade, is a legendary Central European nightshade with a rich history. The plant contains hallucinogenic alkaloids, primarily atropine, which is named after the plant.

Origin and distribution

Atropa belladonna is native to temperate southern, Central, and Eastern Europe, as well as North Africa, Turkey, Iran, and the Caucasus. It has been naturalized in some areas of North America and is considered a weed species in regions with disturbed soils.

Botany

Belladonna, is a plant species characterized by its distinctive features. It grows to a height of approximately 1.5 meters, with a purplish-colored stem. The root system is thick, fleshy, whitish, and branched. The plant's leaves are simple, dark greenish in color, ovate, and alternate in nature. The flowers are solitary and bell-shaped, blooming from June to September. The plant produces berries that are highly toxic, and the seeds contain toxic alkaloids.

Climate and soil

Belladonna is a temperate crop that thrives in deep, fertile soils with medium texture and high humus content. It prefers partial shade and well-drained soils, avoiding heavy clay and waterlogged areas.

Chemical composition

Belladonna contains 0.3-1.0% total alkaloids, primarily l-hyoscyamine and atropine. Other components include apoatropine, scopolamine, and volatile bases. The plant also contains phytosterol, N-methylpyrrolidine, and homatropine.

Varieties

Srinagar: A selection developed by the Regional Research Laboratory, containing 0.6% alkaloid.

Season

Belladonna is typically planted in March-April or October-November.

Land preparation and planting

The crop is propagated through seeds extracted from berries. Seeds are treated with 80% sulfuric acid for 2 minutes to improve germination. Nursery-raised seedlings are transplanted to the field at a spacing of 50-60 cm.

Manures and fertilizers

A basal dose of 25-40 kg N, 40-60 kg P_2O_5, and 30-50 kg K_2O per hectare is recommended, followed by additional doses of 60-80 kg N as top dressing.

Irrigation

Belladonna requires frequent irrigation, ideally once every 10-15 days during dry periods.

Weeding and plant protection

Regular weeding and hoeing are necessary to keep the crop weed-free. Slugs are a common pest, and the plant's poisonous properties make it unsuitable for home gardens.

Harvesting

The first harvest of Belladonna leaves occurs three months after planting, and it's essential to harvest them as soon as the plants start flowering, when the alkaloid content is at its highest. The leaves are carefully cut using pruning scissors. Immediately after harvesting, the leaves are dried under shade, sun, or artificial heat, with or without fans for air circulation. To ensure even drying, the leaves are frequently turned over.

In addition to leaf harvesting, the roots are also harvested after three years. Post-harvest, the roots are washed, cut into 4-inch lengths, and split lengthwise if thick. They are then dried under shade or sun.

Yield

The average yield of dry herb is 600 kg per hectare in the first year, increasing to 1500 kg per hectare in subsequent years. The yield of dry roots varies from 170 to 335 kg per hectare.

MCQ questions

1. What is the scientific name of the Belladonna plant?
   a) *Atropa belladonna* L. b) *Solanum tuberosum* L.
   c) *Piper nigrum* L. d) *Capsicum annuum* L.
2. What is the scientific name of the Belladonna plant?
   a) Solanaceae b) Piperaceae
   c) Rutaceae d) Zingiberaceae
3. What is the primary use of Belladonna in medicine?
   a) As a cosmetic b) As a pain reliever
   c) As an antispasmodic d) As an anti-inflammatory
4. What is the ideal soil type for Belladonna cultivation?
   a) Heavy clay
   b) Sandy loam
   c) Deep fertile soil with medium texture
   d) Waterlogged soil
5. Which part of the Belladonna plant contains the highest amount of alkaloids?
   a) Leaves b) Roots
   c) Flowers d) Fruits
6. How often should Belladonna be irrigated during dry periods?
   a) Once a week b) Once every 10-15 days
   c) Once a month d) Once every 2 months
7. What is the average yield of dry herb per hectare in the first year?
   a) 300 kg b) 600 kg
   c) 900 kg d) 1200 kg
8. Which variety of Belladonna contains 0.6% alkaloid?
   a) Srinagar b) Bella
   c) Atropa d) Shade
9. What is the recommended basal dose of nitrogen per hectare for Belladonna cultivation?
   a) 10-20 kg b) 25-40 kg
   c) 50-60 kg d) 70-80 kg

10. What is the purpose of treating Belladonna seeds with sulfuric acid?
    a) To improve germination
    b) To reduce alkaloid content
    c) To increase yield
    d) To prevent pests

Short answer questions

1. What is the origin of the name "Belladonna"?
2. What are the primary alkaloids present in Belladonna?
3. What is the ideal time for planting Belladonna in the field?
4. How are Belladonna roots harvested and dried?
5. What is the average yield of dry roots per hectare?

Answers for MCQ

1. a) *Atropa belladonna* L.
2. a) Solanaceae
3. c) As an antispasmodic
4. c) Deep fertile soil with medium texture
5. b) Roots
6. b) Once every 10-15 days
7. b) 600 kg
8. a) Srinagar
9. b) 25-40 kg
10. a) To improve germination

References

Akbar, S. and Akbar, S., 2020. Atropa belladonna L.(Solanaceae). Handbook of 200 Medicinal Plants: A Comprehensive Review of Their Traditional Medical Uses and Scientific Justifications, pp.373-379.

Datta, K., 2011. An updated overview on Atropa belladonna L. The International Research Journal of Pharmacy, 2(11), pp.1-7.

Koch, G.P., 1919. The cultivation of medicinal plants. The Journal of the American Pharmaceutical Association (1912), 8(4), pp.275-281.

Merillat, L.A., 1900. Belladonna. The Journal of Comparative Medicine and Veterinary Archives, 21(4), p.198.

Rubika, J., 2014. Atropha belladonna and its Medicinal Uses-A Short Review. Research Journal of Pharmacy and Technology, 7(8), pp.926-930.

4

Cinchona

Scientific name: *Cinchona* spp.

Family: Rubiaceae

Cinchona, a genus of flowering plants, comprises approximately 65 species. Several species, including *Cinchona succirubra*, *C. officinalis*, and *C. ledgeriana*, are cultivated for their bark, which contains quinine and other anti-malarial compounds.

Origin and distribution

Native to the highlands of South America, Cinchona was introduced to India's Nilgiris in 1859. It is currently cultivated in the Anamalai and Nilgiris hills of Tamil Nadu, as well as in Darjeeling, West Bengal.

Botany

Cinchona is a majestic evergreen plant that can grow to varying heights, ranging from 5 to 15 meters. Its trunk is covered with a smooth, greyish-brown bark that peels off in thin layers. The branches are slender, pubescent, and arranged in a whorled pattern.

The leaves of the Cinchona plant are simple, oppositely arranged, and decussate. They are elliptical or lanceolate in shape, with a pointed apex and a rounded base. The leaves are 10-20 cm long, 2-5 cm wide, and have a leathery texture. The upper surface is dark green, glossy, and glabrous, while the lower surface is pale green, pubescent, and has prominent midribs.

The Cinchona plant is also renowned for its stunning blooms, which are a delicate rose or creamy white color. Although tiny in size, these flowers are arranged in terminal clusters, creating a breathtaking display of natural beauty. The flowers are pentamerous, with a funnel-shaped corolla and five stamens. They are also fragrant, emitting a sweet, floral scent.

As the flowers mature, they develop into fruit capsules that contain numerous seeds. The fruit capsules are ovoid, 2-3 cm long, and split open longitudinally to release the seeds. The seeds are small, winged, and wind-dispersed.

Climate and soil

Cinchona thrives in warm, humid environments with well-drained, acidic soil rich in organic matter. Ideal temperatures range from 13.5°C to 21°C, with annual rainfall of at least 200 mm. The plants are sensitive to frost and cannot tolerate extreme temperatures or waterlogging.

Chemical constituents

Cinchona bark contains a range of alkaloids, primarily quinine, quinidine, cinchonine, and cinchonidine. These compounds are responsible for the plant's medicinal properties and are extracted and used to produce various anti-malarial medications.

Varitey

Clone No. 701: This clone was discovered by the Tamil Nadu Forest Department and is known for its high quininc content (approximately 12% quinine sulfate).

Season

The ideal season for cultivating Cinchona is during the spring or early summer months when the weather is warm and humid. In India, the planting season typically falls between March to May or September to November. However, in other regions with similar climatic conditions, the planting season may vary. It is essential to consider factors such as rainfall, temperature, and soil moisture before planting Cinchona. The plant requires adequate rainfall for growth, and planting should be done before the onset of heavy rainfall. Additionally, Cinchona prefers a warm and humid climate, with temperatures ranging from 15°C to 25°C. The soil should be well-drained with adequate moisture, and planting should be done when the soil is moist but not waterlogged.

Land preparation

To prepare the soil, the forest is cleared, and the ground is leveled and excavated to a depth of 1.5 feet to remove stones and improve soil structure. Two weeks prior to planting, 60 x 60 cm trenches are dug and filled with a mixture of topsoil and decomposed organic matter.

Planting material and planting technique

Inchona propagation can be achieved through seeds or vegetative methods. Although seeds are commonly used in India due to their affordability, vegetative propagation is generally preferred. This is because cinchona species often exhibit significant genetic diversity, making vegetative propagation a more reliable method.

To propagate cinchona using seeds, they are typically sown in specially designed beds during the month of April. However, seed viability is short-lived, and only a small percentage of seedlings are suitable for transplantation. Once seedlings have developed two pairs of leaves, they are transplanted and nurtured for approximately 14-18 months before being moved to their final position.

Vegetative propagation methods, including cuttings and grafting, have proven highly effective. One technique, known as patch-budding, boasts an impressive success rate of 85% when performed during the spring months. When transplanting cinchona plants, it is essential to do so before the onset of heavy rainfall. Plants are typically spaced 120-150 cm apart, and shade-providing trees are planted nearby to ensure optimal growing conditions.

Manures and fertilizers

For optimal growth, cinchona plants benefit from the application of a balanced fertilizer mixture containing nitrogen (N), phosphorus (P), and potassium (K). If the soil pH is 5 or lower, liming is necessary to adjust the acidity. The recommended nutrient supply is 115 kg N, 105 kg P2O5, and 115 kg K2O per hectare, typically provided through triple super phosphate, muriate of potash, and ammonium sulphate. Notably, the quinine content in cinchona trees tends to increase with age, provided they receive favourable nutritional conditions.

Plant protection

Cinchona plants are susceptible to various pests and diseases. Tea mosquito bugs (*Helopeltis antonii*) are a common pest that infests leaves in nurseries and main fields, and can be controlled with systemic insecticides.

Diseases affecting cinchona plants include Pythium-induced damping off, seedling blight caused by *Phytophthora palmivora*, and root-rot disease. Other diseases that affect cinchona plants include stripe canker, girdle canker, stem canker, and bleeding disease. Regular monitoring and application of fungicides, such as copper oxy chloride, can help control these diseases.

Harvesting

Cinchona trees are typically coppiced when they are 6-8 years old, depending on their vegetative development. During coppicing, the trees are cut back to 5 cm above the ground, and only 2-3 shoots are retained to grow further. This process is repeated every 8-10 years, and the plants are eventually uprooted after 30 years when their vigor declines.

The major harvest of cinchona bark is obtained during the first two coppicings, with minimal yield from subsequent prunings. The bark is separated from the coppices by beating and peeling, and then dried immediately to prevent alkaloid loss. Drying methods include shade drying, designated sheds, artificial heating, and controlled ovens. The dried bark is then broken into small pieces, packed into gunny bags, and traded as "Druggists' bark" with a quinine content of 1.8-2%.

Yield

Cinchona plantations yield approximately 4000 kg of dry stem bark per hectare during the first two coppicing cycles. At the final stage, when the trees are uprooted, the yield increases to around 6000 kg/ha.

Processing and extraction

The dried bark is ground into a powder, mixed with slaked lime, and extracted with solvents. The alkaloids are then isolated, purified, and converted into various quinine salts. This process involves several stages, including:

Grinding: The dried bark is ground into a fine powder to increase its surface area.

Mixing with alkali: The powdered bark is mixed with slaked lime to create a uniformly moist slurry.

Extraction: The alkaloids are extracted from the bark using solvents such as amyl alcohol or ether.

Purification: The extracted alkaloids are purified and converted into various quinine salts.

Commercial extraction

Two Indian facilities, the Government Quinine Factory in West Bengal and the Government Quinine Factory in Tamil Nadu, are involved in the commercial extraction of Cinchona alkaloids. The process involves grinding the bark, mixing it with alkali, extracting the alkaloids with solvents, and purifying the extracted compounds. The extracted quinine is then used to produce various anti-malarial medications.

MCQ questions

1. What is the primary use of Cinchona bark?
   a) To produce quinine and other anti-malarial compounds
   b) To produce tea and other beverages
   c) To produce spices and other flavorings
   d) To produce dyes and other coloring agents

2. Where was Cinchona introduced in India in 1859?

a) Nilgiris b) Darjeeling
c) Anamalai d) Tamil Nadu

3. What is the ideal temperature range for Cinchona cultivation?

a) 10°C - 15°C b) 13.5°C - 21°C
c) 20°C - 25°C d) 25°C - 30°C

4. What is the primary alkaloid extracted from Cinchona bark?

a) Quinine b) Quinidine
c) Cinchonine d) Cinchonidine

5. How often is the bark harvested from Cinchona plants?

a) Every 2-3 years b) Every 6-8 years
c) Every 10-12 years d) Every 15-20 years

6. What is the purpose of mixing Cinchona bark with slaked lime?

a) To extract alkaloids b) To remove impurities
c) To improve texture d) To increase yield

7. Which of the following is a commercial producer of quinine from Cinchona bark?

a) Government Quinine Factory, West Bengal
b) Government Quinine Factory, Tamil Nadu
c) Both A and B
d) Neither A nor B

8. What is the name of the disease caused by Phytophthora palmivora in Cinchona plants?

a) Seedling blight b) Root rot
c) Stripe canker d) Girdle canker

9. How is the extracted quinine purified and converted into various salts?

a) Through recrystallization b) Through distillation
c) Through filtration d) Through centrifugation

10. What is the recommended spacing between Cinchona plants?

a) 60-90 cm b) 120-150 cm
c) 180-200 cm d) 250-300 cm

Short answer questions

1. What are the primary species of Cinchona cultivated for their bark?
2. Describe the process of extracting alkaloids from Cinchona bark.
3. What are the ideal soil conditions for Cinchona cultivation?
4. What is the purpose of coppicing in Cinchona cultivation?
5. What are the primary uses of quinine extracted from Cinchona bark?

Answers for MCQ

1. a) To produce quinine and other anti-malarial compounds
2. a) Nilgiris
3. b) 13.5°C - 21°C
4. a) Quinine
5. b) Every 6-8 years
6. a) To extract alkaloids
7. c) Both A and B
8. a) Seedling blight
9. a) Through recrystallization
10. b) 120 -150 cm

References

Aslam, S., Jabeen, T., Ahmad, M. and AL-Huqail, A.A., 2023. In Essentials of Medicinal and Aromatic Crops (pp. 221-248). Cham: Springer International Publishing.

Gorkom, K.W., 1883. A Handbook of Cinchona Culture. JH de Bussy.

Gupta, R., 2017. Agrotechnology of medicinal plants. In The medicinal plant industry (pp. 43-58). Routledge.

Nair, K.P. and Nair, K.P., 2021. Cinchona (Cinchona sp.). Tree Crops: Harvesting Cash from the World's Important Cash Crops, pp.129-151.

Popenoe, W., 1949. Cinchona cultivation in Guatemala - a brief historical review up to 1943. Economic Botany, 3(2), pp.150-157.

5

Greater Yam

Scientific name: *Dioscorea alata* L.

Family: Dioscoreaceae

Dioscorea alata, commonly known as water yam or purple yam, is a species of yam belonging to the family Dioscoreaceae. Native to Southeast Asia, this tropical and subtropical crop has gained popularity worldwide for its edible, nutrient-rich tubers. The plant's unique characteristic is its purple-colored tubers, which owe their distinct hue to anthocyanins, powerful antioxidants that provide numerous health benefits. With its exceptional nutritional profile, Dioscorea alata has become an attractive alternative to other tubers, offering a valuable addition to various culinary dishes.

Origin and distribution

Dioscorea alata, a yam species, exhibits a widespread geographical distribution, with its origin tracing back to Southeast Asia. Phylogeographical studies indicate that the species has undergone extensive dispersal and cultivation, resulting in its presence globally in tropical and subtropical regions. Notably, *D. alata* has become naturalized in the southeastern United States, the Caribbean, and parts of Africa, where it is widely cultivated for its edible tubers.

Botany

Dioscorea alata L., commonly known as Purple yam, is a twining, herbaceous vine that grows up to 10 meters in length. The stem is slender, cylindrical, and woody at the base, covered with smooth, glabrous skin that is often purple or reddish-brown in color. The leaves are alternate, simple, and cordate (heart-shaped) with a pointed apex, measuring 5-15 cm long and 3-8 cm wide. They have a smooth, glabrous surface, entire leaf margins, and a long, slender petiole.

The inflorescence is a spike or panicle that grows up to 30 cm long, bearing small, greenish-yellow flowers. The flowers are unisexual, with male and female flowers occurring on different plants (dioecious). The male flowers are smaller, with 6 tepals and 6 stamens, while the female flowers have 6 tepals and a 3-locular ovary. The fruit is a capsule that is 2-3 cm long and 1-2 cm wide, dehiscent and splitting open to release several seeds.

The tubers, which are the edible part of the plant, are formed on the roots. They are cylindrical or oval in shape, with a rough, scaly skin that is often purple or reddish-brown in color. The flesh is white, yellow, or purple, and is rich in starch. The roots are fibrous, with several tubers forming on the root system.

Climate and soil

Dioscorea alata thrives in warm, humid tropical environments with temperatures around 30°C and annual rainfall of 1200-2000mm. The plantrequires specific soil and climate conditions to thrive. It prefers well-drained, loamy soil rich in organic matter, with a slightly acidic to neutral pH ranging from 5.5 to 6.5. The soil should be moist but not waterlogged, and good drainage is essential to prevent tuber rot.

Chemical compounds

The plant is a rich source of valuable and healthy secondary metabolites. The key bioactive compounds present include phenolic acids, flavonoids, anthocyanins, diosgenin (a steroidal sapogenin), saponins, polysaccharides, muco-polysaccharides, proteins, amino acids, and polyphenols. These phytochemicals contribute to the medicinal and nutritional value, making it a valuable crop for human consumption.

Varieties

Sree Keerthi, Sree Roopa, Sree Shilpa, Sree Karthika, Sree Swathy, Sree Neelima, Sree Nidhi and Sree Hima are varieties related to Central Tuber Crops Research Institute, Sreekaryam. Indu is a variety released from Kerala Agricultural University.

Season

In India, the ideal time for planting seed tubers of Dioscorea alata is during the late dry season, typically in March and April. This allows the tubers to sprout with the onset of the southwest monsoon, which provides optimal moisture conditions for growth and development.

Land preparation

To prepare the field for planting *Dioscorea alata*, the field is first ploughed to a fine tilth to loosen the soil and remove any debris. Ridges and furrows are then created at a spacing of 75 cm. Next, pits measuring 45 x 45 x 45 cm are dug, spaced 1 x 1 m apart. The pits are then filled with a mixture of topsoil and cattle manure or compost, creating a nutrient-rich environment for the seed tubers to grow.

Planting material and planting technique

Dioscorea alata can be propagated through single node leaf cuttings, tuber division, or planting tuber pieces. Mature tubers or pieces of tubers from the previous crop are used as planting material. Small tubers are cut into 2-4 sections, while larger ones are divided into 6-8 sections, each containing 2-3 dormant buds. Before planting, the tuber pieces are left in the sun for a few hours to promote wound healing and reduce the risk of fungal infection. Dioscorea alata can be intercropped with other plants like coconut, rubber, banana, areca nut, and coffee at a spacing of 90x90 cm, with a seeding rate of 1875-2500 kg/ha.

Irrigation

Dioscorea alata requires adequate moisture, especially during the growing stage. Copious watering once a week is necessary during dry periods, while during the rainy season, no irrigation is needed, as the rainfall provides sufficient moisture.

Manures and fertilizer

For optimal growth and development, *Dioscorea alata* requires the application of organic and inorganic fertilizers. Cattle manure or compost is applied as basal dose at 10-15 tonnes/ha. An NPK dose of 80:60:80 kg/ha is also applied in two split doses. The first split dose, applied within one week after sprouting, consists of half the nitrogen and potassium dose and the full dose of phosphorus. The remaining half dose of nitrogen and potassium is applied one month later, along with weeding and earthing up.

Weeding

Effective weeding is crucial for the healthy growth and development of Dioscorea alata. The critical period for weeding is between the 8th and 16th week after planting, during which weeding should be done at least three times. Hand weeding is the most efficient method, allowing for precise removal of weeds. Moreover, a targeted weeding strategy focusing on weeds that can host pathogens can significantly reduce the risk of diseases.

Plant protection

Yam scale is a common issue affecting alata tubers in both storage and field conditions. To prevent this, planting materials can be treated with a recommended pesticide. Using scale-free seed tubers for planting is also an effective preventive strategy. Additionally, yams with bruises should be cured and dipped in wood ash to prevent fungal rot. Implementing crop protection measures can also help control nematodes.

Harvesting

The crop will be ready for harvest when its leaves and vines turn brown and dry up. Manual harvesting using digging sticks or wooden spades is the usual practice, with careful handling to avoid tuber damage. The maturity period varies from 8-10 months, depending on the variety.

Yeild

Dioscorea alata has a promising yield potential, producing approximately 20-25 tonnes per hectare within a cultivation period of 240 days.

Postharvest handling

Fresh yam tubers are processed into flour through a series of steps. First, the tubers are peeled and sliced, then boiled in water until partly cooked. The boiling time depends on the thickness of the slices. The partly cooked slices are then dried in a dryer. Finally, the dried yam slices are milled into flour.

MCQ questions

1. What is the common name of *Dioscorea alata*?
   a) Water yam or Purple yam b) Greater yam or White yam
   c) Lesser yam or Wild yam d) Sweet yam or Yellow yam
2. Where is *Dioscorea alata native* to?
   a) Southeast Asia b) Africa
   c) South America d) North America
3. What is the ideal time for planting *Dioscorea alata* in India?
   a) January-February b) March-April
   c) May-June d) July-August
4. How is *Dioscorea alata* typically propagated?
   a) Single node leaf cuttings b) Tuber division
   c) Planting tuber pieces d) All of the above
5. What is the recommended spacing for planting Dioscorea alata?
   a) 60x60 cm b) 90x90 cm
   c) 120x120 cm d) 150x150 cm
6. How often should Dioscorea alata be watered during dry periods?
   a) Daily b) Every other day
   c) Once a week d) Once a month

7. What is the recommended basal dose of cattle manure or compost for Dioscorea alata?

   a) 5-10 tonnes/ha
   b) 10-15 tonnes/ha
   c) 15-20 tonnes/ha
   d) 20-25 tonnes/ha

8. When is the critical period for weeding Dioscorea alata?

   a) 1st-4th week after planting
   b) 8th-16th week after planting
   c) 20th-24th week after planting
   d) 28th-32nd week after planting

9. How long does it take for Dioscorea alata to mature?

   a) 6-8 months
   b) 8-10 months
   c) 10-12 months
   d) 12-14 months

10. What is the approximate yield potential of Dioscorea alata?

    a) 10-15 tonnes/ha
    b) 15-20 tonnes/ha
    c) 20-25 tonnes/ha
    d) 25-30 tonnes/ha

Short answer questions

1. Explain soil and climate conditions for Dioscorea alata
2. Give an account on the cultivation practices for Dioscorea alata
3. Explain method of harvesting
4. Post harvesting technologies and value additions forDioscorea alata
5. Describe the chemical constituents in Dioscorea alata
6. Explain the method of manuring and land preparation in Dioscorea alata crops

Answers for MCQ

1. a) Water yam or Purple yam
2. a) Southeast Asia
3. b) March-April
4. d) All of the above
5. b) 90x90 cm
6. c) Once a week
7. b) 10-15 tonnes/ha
8. b) 8-16 weeks after planting
9. b) 8-10 months
10. c) 20-25 tonnes/ha

References

Abraham, K. and Gopinathan Nair, P., 1990. Floral biology and artificial pollination in Dioscorea alata L. Euphytica, 48, pp.45-51.

Akoroda, M.O., 1993. Yams: Dioscorea spp. In Genetic improvement of vegetable crops (pp. 717-733). Pergamon.

Bhattacharjee, R., Gedil, M., Sartie, A., Otoo, E., Dumet, D., Kikuno, H., Kumar, P.L. and Asiedu, R., 2011. Dioscorea. Wild Crop Relatives: Genomic and Breeding Resources: Industrial Crops, pp.71-96.

Cabrera, M., Gómez, R., Espinosa, E., López, J., Medero, V., Basail, M. and Santos, A., 2011. Yam (Dioscorea alata L.) microtuber formation in Temporary Immersion System as planting material. Biotecnología Aplicada, 28(4), pp.268-271.

Wilson, L.A., 2019. Dioscorea. In Handbook of Flowering (pp. 450-454). CRC Press.

6

Isabgol

Scientific name: *Plantago ovata* Forsk.

Family: Plantaginaceae

Isabgol, or Psyllium husk or Blond psyllium, belongs to the family Plantaginaceae. This medicinal herb has been used for centuries in India, particularly for its seed's therapeutic properties. The name "Isabgol" originates from Persian, with "Isab" meaning horse and "Gol" meaning ear, describing the seed's distinctive shape.

Isabgol is cultivated globally and is valued for its medicinal and industrial applications. The seed's medicinal properties make it an effective remedy for constipation and digestive issues. Additionally, Isabgol is used in the food industry to produce various products, such as candies, biscuits, and ice cream.

Origin and distribution

Isabgol *(Plantago ovata)* is native to the Mediterranean region, West Asia, and parts of Pakistan, including Sindh and Sutleg. Its distribution also extends to the Canary Islands, Southern Spain, the Middle East, North Africa, and North-Western Asia.

Botany

It is 10-15 cm tall short-stemmed annual herb. Flowers in terminal spikes; fruit is a capsule. Theflowers are white in colour and minute. It is highly self-pollinated. The capsule is ovate, 8 mmlong, releasing the smooth, dull, ovate seeds. The seeds are covered with a translucent membrane, known as the husk. The husked seeds are dark red and hard.

Climatic and soil requirements

Isabgol is highly sensitive to environmental factors, necessitating a cool climate and dry, sunny conditions during maturation. Temperatures between 20-25°C are optimal for seed germination, while temperatures ranging from 30-35°C are required for maturity.

The crop thrives in well-drained, light sandy to sandy loam soils. Additionally, it can be cultivated on clay loam, heavy black soils, and medium black cotton soils, provided good drainage is ensured. Regions with winter rains are not suitable for Isabgol cultivation due to the risk of seed shedding and reduced yields.

Chemical constituents

Isabgol's chemical composition is characterized by the presence of various constituents. The protein content is approximately 0.94%, comprising globuline, prolamine, and albamine. Additionally, isabgol contains a significant amount of hemicelluloses, which are polysaccharides with a xylan backbone linked with arabinose, rhamnose, and arabinoxylans.

The mucilage of isabgol is composed of a single polysaccharide containing D-galacturonic acid, D-xylose, L-arabinose, and L-rhamnose. The ash content of isabgol is approximately 4.07%. Furthermore, isabgol also contains various secondary metabolites, including iridoid glycosides, terpinoids, phenolics, and flavonoids.

Varieties

Several improved varieties of isabgol have been developed for commercial cultivation. ICAR-DMAPR has developed eight varieties: GI 2, GI 3, HI-5, RI-1, VI-1, VI-2, and VI-3. Additionally, CSIR-CIMAP Lucknow has released a variety named "Niharika".

Season

The optimal time for sowing isabgol seeds is between the last week of October and the first week of November. Sowing during this period allows for ideal germination and growth conditions. Notably, sowing isabgol in the first week of November has been observed to yield the best results, making it the most recommended sowing time for optimal yields.

Land preparation

To facilitate optimal seed germination, it is essential to prepare a fine tilth. This involves ploughing and harrowing the land according to the soil's condition. Additionally, the field should be subdivided into smaller plots, typically measuring 8-12 meters in length and 3 meters in width, taking into account the soil type and slope.

Planting material and planting technique

Isabgol is typically propagated through seeds, with a recommended seeding rate of 3-4 kg/ha. The optimal sowing period is from November to mid-December. Seeds are sown using the direct broadcasting method, followed by light sweeping with a tree twig or broom, taking care to ensure seeds are not deeply buried to facilitate uniform germination. For optimal propagation, bold, disease-free seeds from the previous year's crop are recommended.

Irrigation

Isabgol requires light irrigation with a slow flow immediately after sowing. In cases of poor germination, a second irrigation is necessary. The irrigation schedule varies depending on soil type, with sandy loam soils requiring three irrigations: one at sowing, one 30 days after sowing, and another 70 days after sowing. The final irrigation should coincide with the milk stage of the majority of spikes. In dry, light soils, additional irrigations may be necessary. Notably, isabgol can tolerate low levels of salinity, allowing for the use of low-concentration saline water for irrigation purposes.

Manuring

Isabgol has a low nitrogen requirement, and inorganic nitrogen is applied only when the soil nitrogen content falls below 120 kg/ha. The recommended fertilizer application rates for optimal growth are 20-30 kg/ha of nitrogen and 15-25 kg/ha of phosphorus. The fertilizer application schedule involves applying the full dose of phosphorus and half of the nitrogen with the last ploughing, and top-dressing the remaining nitrogen 40 days after sowing.

Weeding

The isabgol crop requires 2-3 weedings during its growing period. Hand weeding and interculturing are effective methods for controlling weeds, which in turn helps to increase both the yield and quality of the isabgol crop.

Plant protection

The major disease affecting isabgol is Downy Mildew, which can be controlled by treating seeds with metalaxyl and spraying 0.2% metalaxyl at disease onset. Aphid is another major pest that appears 50-60 days after sowing and can be managed with two sprays of 0.02% oxydemeton methyl, 12-15 days apart. To avoid seed loss, slightly unripe spikes are harvested, especially if unseasonal rain is expected, and spraying of insecticides and fungicides is stopped 45 days before harvesting to avoid pesticide residue issues.

Harvest

Isabgol spikes are harvested after 10 AM, once the morning dew has dried. Plants are cut at ground level or uprooted if the soil is loose. Harvested plants are then collected in a clean threshing yard. To minimize seed loss due to shattering, slightly unripe spikes are harvested, especially if there's a risk of unseasonal rain.

Yield

In Gujarat, the average seed yield of isabgol is typically around 800-1000 kg/ha. However, higher seed yields can be achieved with favorable weather conditions and improved management practices.

Postharvest handling

After harvesting, the isabgol seeds are separated from the plant material through trampling, using either bullocks or tractors. The seeds then undergo processing through a series of grinding mills to remove the husk, resulting in a 30% husk recovery rate by weight. Threshing is done using a tractor or motor-operated threshing machine. The resulting straw is collected and utilized as fodder for farm animals.

MCQ questions

1. What is the botanical name of Isabgol?
   a) Plantago ovata b) Plantago major
   c) Plantago lanceolata d) Plantago psyllium
2. Which part of the Isabgol plant is used for medicinal purposes?
   a) Leaves b) Roots
   c) Seeds d) Stem
3. What is the recommended sowing time for Isabgol in India?
   a) Last week of September b) Last week of October
   c) First week of November d) First week of December
4. What is the average seed yield of Isabgol in Gujarat?
   a) 500-700 kg/ha b) 800-1000 kg/ha
   c) 1200-1500 kg/ha d) 1800-2000 kg/ha
5. What is the main disease affecting Isabgol?
   a) Powdery mildew b) Downy mildew
   c) Leaf spot d) Root rot
6. What is the recommended fertilizer application rate for Isabgol?
   a) 10-20 kg/ha of nitrogen and 10-15 kg/ha of phosphorus
   b) 20-30 kg/ha of nitrogen and 15-25 kg/ha of phosphorus
   c) 30-40 kg/ha of nitrogen and 20-30 kg/ha of phosphorus
   d) 40-50 kg/ha of nitrogen and 25-35 kg/ha of phosphorus

7. What is the purpose of threshing in Isabgol cultivation?
   a) To separate seeds from plant material
   b) To remove husk from seeds
   c) To dry the seeds
   d) To pack the seeds
8. What is the recommended method for controlling weeds in Isabgol?
   a) Hand weeding and interculturing
   b) Chemical weeding
   c) Mechanical weeding
   d) Biological weeding
9. What is the name of the variety of Isabgol released by CSIR-CIMAP Lucknow?
   a) Niharika b) Isabgol-1
   c) Psyllium-1 d) GI-2
10. What is the percentage of husk recovered from Isabgol seeds?
   a) 20-25% b) 25-30%
   c) 30-35% d) 35-40%

Short answer questions

1. Explain soil and climate conditions for Isabgol
2. Give an account on the cultivation practices for Isabgol
3. Explain method of harvesting
4. Post harvesting technologies and value additions forIsabgol
5. Describe the chemical constituents in Isabgol

Answers for MCQ

1. a) *Plantago ovata*
2. c) Seeds
3. c) First week of November
4. b) 800-1000 kg/ha
5. b) Downy mildew
6. b) 20-30 kg/ha of nitrogen and 15-25 kg/ha of phosphorus
7. a) To separate seeds from plant material
8. a) Hand weeding and interculturing
9. a) Niharika
10. b) 30% (by weight)

References

Akbar, S. and Akbar, S., 2020. Plantago ovata Forssk.(Plantaginaceae) (Syn.: P. ispaghula Roxb. ex Fleming). Handbook of 200 Medicinal Plants: A Comprehensive Review of Their Traditional Medical Uses and Scientific Justifications, pp.1465-1473.

Khaliq, R., Tita, O., Antofie, M.M. and Sava, C., 2015. Industrial application of psyllium: an overview. Acta Universitatis Cibiniensis. Technical Series, 67(1), pp.210-214.

Masood, R. and Miraftab, M., 2010. Psyllium: current and future applications. In Medical and healthcare textiles (pp. 244-253). Woodhead Publishing.

Sarfraz, R.M., Khan, H., Maheen, S., Afzal, S., Akram, M.R., Mahmood, A., Afzal, K., Abrar, M.A., Akram, M.A., Andaleeb, M. and Haider, I., 2017. Plantago ovata: A comprehensive review on cultivation, bio-chemical, pharmaceutical and pharmacological aspects. Acta poloniae pharmaceutica, 74(3), pp.739-746.

Verma, A. and Mogra, R., 2013. Psyllium (Plantago ovata)husk: a wonder food for good health. International Journal of Science and Research, 4(9), pp.1581-1585.

7

Long pepper

Scientific name: *Piper longum L.*

Family: Piperaceae

Piper longum, commonly known as long pepper, is a flowering vine native to the tropical regions of India, Southeast Asia, and Sri Lanka. It has been used for centuries in traditional medicine, particularly in Ayurveda and Unani systems, for its numerous health benefits. The plant is characterized by its slender stems, heart-shaped leaves, and spikes of small flowers. The fruit of the plant, a small, elongated berry, is the part commonly used for medicinal and culinary purposes.

Origin and distribution

The plant is native to South and Southeast Asia. The wild type of *Piper longum* is mainly found in Kerala, Assam, West Bengal, Nepal, Uttar Pradesh, Andhra Pradesh, and the North East region. The plant is cultivated in various parts of India, including Bengal, Assam, Maharashtra, Tamil Nadu, Orissa, and Meghalaya. *Piper longum* naturally occurs in the central Himalayas to Assam, Khasi and Mikir hills, and the evergreen forests of Western Ghats from Konkan to Kanyakumari and Nicobar Island.

Botany

Long Pepper is a perennial climber belonging to the family Piperaceae. It is native to the tropical regions of India, Southeast Asia, and the Pacific Islands. The plant grows up to 1.5 meters in height, with a thick, woody stem that climbs on nearby supports using its adventitious roots. The leaves are alternate, simple, and cordate, with a pointed apex and a heart-shaped base, measuring 5-10 cm in length. The inflorescence is a spike, bearing small, white, and unisexual flowers that are arranged spirally. The fruit is a small, berry-like drupe, containing a single seed, which is the edible part of the plant, commonly known as Long Pepper or Pippali. The plant prefers well-drained soil, partial shade, and a warm, humid climate, making it an ideal crop for tropical regions.

Climate and soil

The crop requires specific climatic conditions to thrive. It is typically cultivated in high rainfall areas without supplemental irrigation and needs high humidity and frequent irrigation due to its shallow roots. The plant grows best under partial shade and can be intercropped with coconut and areca nut plantations. However, it is highly sensitive to drought and waterlogging conditions. In terms of soil requirements, *Piper longum* can thrive in a variety of soils, but light, porous, well-drained soils rich in organic content provide the ideal conditions for its cultivation.

Chemical compounds

Long pepper contains a diverse array of bioactive compounds. The fruit is rich in volatile oil, resin, and alkaloids, including piperine (4-5%) and a terpinoid substance. The root, in particular, contains piperlongumine as a major alkaloid, along with piperine. Various parts of the plant have yielded a range of constituents, including piperine, piperlongumine, and sesamin. Notably, the roots of long pepper have been found to contain piperine, piperlongumine, and tetrahydropiperlongumine, among other compounds. Recent studies have also identified novel compounds, such as piperoic acid and guineesine, which contribute to the plant's medicinal properties.

Varieties

The "Viswam" variety of *Piper longum* is a promising cultivar, particularly suited for intercropping. This variety attains a height of 72 cm and has a prolonged flowering stage. The plant bears stout, short, thick spikes with a dark green color, with a dry matter content of approximately 20%. The "Viswam" variety provides an economic yield within 240-270 days per year, with the spikes containing around 2.80% alkaloids

Land preparation

To cultivate *Piper longum*, prepare the land with 2-3 ploughings, followed by harrowing and levelling. Ensure proper drainage to prevent waterlogging.

Planting material and planting techniques

Use rooted vine cuttings with 2-3 nodes for planting. Rooting takes 15-20 days. Plant in May-June, with 60x60 cm spacing.

Irrigation

Irrigate during summer, once or twice a week, depending on soil type. Apply irrigation during monsoon if rainfall is scarce.

Manuring

In the first year, apply about 20 ton per hector FYM at the time of land preparation. In the subsequent years, apply FYM before the onset of monsoon.

Plant protection

Monitoring for mealy bugs and tea mosquitoes is essential to protect Piper longum plants from pests. Mealy bugs form colonies on roots and stems, causing yellowing and stunted growth, especially during summer. Tea mosquitoes, on the other hand, feed on foliage, leading to damage. To manage these pests, spraying 2.5% Neem kernel suspension is recommended, providing an effective and eco-friendly solution.

Harvest

Plants typically begin fruiting six months after planting, with female spikes maturing in about two months. Harvesting occurs before the spikes ripen, when they turn a distinctive blackish-green color, indicating peak pungency. Hand-picking is preferred, followed by sun drying for 7-10 days. In Kerala, three to four harvests can be made, yielding 400 kg/ha in the first year and up to 1000 kg/ha by the third year. However, yields decline after the third year, and plants become uneconomical by the fifth year. The entire plant is harvested at this stage by cutting the stem at ground level and digging up the roots. The harvested roots are then cut into 2.5-5 cm lengths, dried, and sold as piplamool.

Postharvest handling

To preserve the quality of dried Piper longum spikes, store them in airtight, moisture-proof containers.

MCQ questions

1. What is the scientific name of the long pepper plant?
   a) *Piper nigrum* b) *Piper longum*
   c) *Piper officinarum* d) *Piper cubeba*
2. Which of the following is a traditional medicine system that uses *Piper longum*?
   a) Ayurveda b) Unani
   c) Homeopathy d) All of the above
3. What is the ideal climate for cultivating *Piper longum*?
   a) High temperature and low humidity
   b) Low temperature and high humidity
   c) High rainfall and high humidity
   d) Low rainfall and low humidity

4. Which part of the *Piper longum* plant is commonly used for medicinal purposes?
   a) Roots b) Stems
   c) Leaves d) Fruits
5. What is the name of the promising cultivar of *Piper longum*?
   a) Viswam b) Piperine
   c) Long pepper d) Piplamool
6. How often should *Piper longum* plants be irrigated during summer?
   a) Daily b) Once or twice a week
   c) Once a month d) Never
7. What is the recommended method for managing mealy bug infestations in *Piper longum* plants?
   a) Spraying chemical pesticides
   b) Spraying 2.5% Neem kernel suspension
   c) Hand-picking the bugs
   d) Using sticky traps
8. At what stage are *Piper longum* spikes typically harvested?
   a) When they turn red
   b) When they turn blackish-green
   c) When they turn yellow
   d) When they turn brown
9. How long does it take for *Piper longum* plants to begin fruiting after planting?
   a) 3 months b) 6 months
   c) 9 months d) 1 year
10. What is the average yield of dried *Piper longum* spikes per hectare in the first year?
   a) 200 kg b) 400 kg
   c) 600 kg d) 800 kg

Short answer questions

1. Explain soil and climate conditions for Piper longum
2. Give an account on the cultivation practices for Piper longum
3. Explain method of harvesting
4. Post harvesting technologies and value additions for Piper longum
5. Describe the chemical constituents in Piper longum

Answers for MCQ

1. b) Piper longum
2. d) All of the above (Ayurveda, Unani, and other traditional medicine systems)
3. c) High rainfall and high humidity
4. a) Roots (and fruits, but roots are more commonly used)
5. a) Viswam
6. b) Once or twice a week
7. b) Spraying 2.5% Neem kernel suspension
8. b) When they turn blackish-green
9. b) 6 months
10. b) 400 kg

References

Babu, K.N., Divakaran, M., Ravindran, P.N. and Peter, K.V. (2006) Long pepper. In Handbook of herbs and spices, pp. 420-437. Woodhead Publishing.

Joshi, K., Panara, K., Nishteswar, K. and Chaudhary, S. (2013) Cultivation and pharmacological profiles of root of Piper longum Linn. Pharma Science Monitor, 4(1).

Manoj, P., Soniya, E.V., Banerjee, N.S. and Ravichandran, P. (2004) Recent studies on well-known spice, Piper longum Linn.

Peter, K.V. (2006) Long pepper. Handbook of herbs and spices, p. 420.

Sharangi, A.B., Datta, S. and Deb, P. (2018) Spices: Agrotechniques for Quality Produce. CRC Press.

8

Periwinkle

Scientific name: *Catharanthus roseus* (L.) G.Don

Family: Apocyanaceae

Catharanthus roseus (*Vinca rose*a)is a perennial flowering plant in the family Apocyanaceae. It is commonly known as Cape periwinkle, Madagascar periwinkle or graveyard plant etc. Periwinkle is an extensively investigated medicinal plant after the discovery of powerful anticancer alkaloids such as Vinblastine and Vincristine, in its leaves more than 50 years ago. These alkaloids have revolutionized cancer treatment and saved countless lives worldwide. Today, Catharanthus roseus remains a vital source of inspiration for cancer research and drug development.

Origin and distribution

Periwinkle is native and endemic to Madagascar. However, it is now cultivated and grown in many tropical and subtropical regions worldwide, including the southern United States, West Indies, and several states in India, such as Karnataka, Tamil Nadu, and Gujarat. Unfortunately, the plant is endangered in its natural habitat due to habitat destruction and burn and slash agriculture.

Botany

Periwinkle is a perennial herb belonging to the Apocynaceae family. It is a popular ornamental plant, often grown in gardens for its attractive pink and white flowers that bloom throughout the year. The plant has a spreading habit, with flexible, long branches that bear simple, opposite leaves. These leaves are elliptical to ovate in shape, measuring 2.5-5 cm in length and 1-2 cm in width, with a glossy, dark green appearance and a pointed tip.

The inflorescence of Periwinkle consists of cymes, with 2-3 flowers in axillary and terminal clusters. The flowers themselves are salver-shaped, with a pink or white corolla featuring five fused petals and a purple center. They measure 2-3 cm in diameter and bloom throughout the year, adding to the plant's ornamental value. The fruit of Periwinkle is a cylindrical follicle, 2-4 cm long and 0.5-1 cm wide, containing many black seeds.

In terms of its vegetative structure, Periwinkle has a herbaceous stem that is green and slightly woody at the base. The stem has a milky sap that flows when cut. The roots of the plant are fibrous and spread out in all directions, anchoring the plant firmly in the soil. Overall, Periwinkle is a versatile and attractive plant with a range of uses beyond its ornamental value.

Climate and soil

In terms of climate, Periwinkle flourishes in tropical and subtropical areas. It can even grow in subtropical regions of Northern India, although growth may be slower due to extremely low winter temperatures. Adequate rainfall, with a well-distributed annual rainfall of 100cm or more, is ideal for the plant's growth.

Periwinkle is adaptable to various climate and soil conditions. It thrives best in well-drained, moist soil rich in humus. The plant can tolerate a range of soils, including sand, clay, loam, and acidic to slightly alkaline soils with a pH of 5.5-6. However, it cannot grow in highly saline, alkaline, or waterlogged soils.

Chemical composition

Periwinkle is a rich source of bioactive compounds, including a group of toxic alkaloids that have been found to have anticancer properties. The plant contains a diverse range of phytochemicals, including carbohydrates, saponins, flavanoids, tannins, terpinoids, steroids, and over 400 types of alkaloids. Notable alkaloids present in the aerial parts of the plant include actine plastidemeric, vinblastine, vindesine, and vincristine, while the roots and basal stem contain alkaloids such as vinceine, vineamine, ajmalicine, and catharanthine. Additionally, the flowers of Catharanthus roseus contain a unique anthocyanine pigment called Rosindin.

Varieties

Two improved varieties of Periwinkle, "Nirmal" and "Dhawal", have been developed by the Central Institute of Medicinal and Aromatic Plants (CIMAP). These varieties exhibit a high level of field resistance to the die-back disease, making them more resilient and suitable for cultivation.

Season

The ideal season for cultivating Periwinkle varies depending on the region. In tropical regions, it can be cultivated throughout the year. In subtropical regions, the best times for cultivation are during the spring (February-March) and autumn (September-October). In temperate regions, summer (June-July) is the most suitable time for cultivating Periwinkle.

Land preparation

The land should be ploughed 2-3 times to a depth of 20-25 cm to break clods and remove weeds. Then, the soil should be leveled and formed into raised beds. The beds should be 10-15 cm high and 1-1.5 meters wide. This helps improve drainage and aeration, essential for healthy root growth and plant development.

Planting material and planting technique

Periwinkle plants can be propagated through two methods:

Stem Cutting: 4-6 inch stem sections with leaves are cut, dipped in rooting powder, and planted in pots with a perlite-sand-peat moss mixture.

Seed Propagation: Fresh seeds are directly sown during the monsoon season, with 2.5 kg/ha, mixed with moist sand for even distribution.

Manure and fertilizer

For optimal growth, Periwinkle benefits from fertilizers with a balanced NPK ratio. To begin, the soil is enriched with a combination of 250kg of superphosphate and 65kg of muriate of potash. Additionally, 110kg of urea is split into two applications: one 10-15 days after transplanting and the second a month later. This fertilizer plan is ideal for irrigated crops; however, the fertilizer and manure quantities should be reduced by half for crops relying on rainfall.

Irrigation

Periwinkle plants require irrigation in areas with seasonal monsoons. Typically, 4-5 irrigations are done at 15-day intervals during February, March, and April.

Weeding

Weeding is done twice: first after 60 days from sowing or transplanting and again after an additional 60 days.

Plant protection

Periwinkle plants are generally resilient but can be susceptible to pests and diseases like aphids, spider mites, powdery mildew, and "little leaf" disease.

Harvesting and postharvest management

The crop is harvested after 12 months from sowing. The plant is cut 7.5cm above the ground, dried in shade, and then roots are collected after irrigation and ploughing.

MCQ questions

1. What is the scientific name of Periwinkle?
   a) *Catharanthus roseus* b) *Vinca rosea*
   c) *Apocynaceae roseus* d) *Madagascar periwinkle*
2. Which part of the Periwinkle plant contains anticancer alkaloids?
   a) Leaves b) Roots
   c) Flowers d) Stem
3. What is the ideal annual rainfall for Periwinkle cultivation?
   a) 50 cm b) 100 cm
   c) 150 cm d) 200 cm
4. Which of the following is a notable alkaloid present in Periwinkle?
   a) Vinblastine b) Vincristine
   c) Ajmalicine d) All of the above
5. What is the name of the unique anthocyanine pigment found in Periwinkle flowers?
   a) Rosindin b) Vinblastine
   c) Vincristine d) Catharanthine
6. Which institute developed the improved varieties of Periwinkle, "Nirmal" and "Dhawal"?
   a) CIMAP b) ICAR
   c) ICMR d) CSIR
7. What is the ideal season for cultivating Periwinkle in tropical regions?
   a) Spring b) Summer
   c) Autumn d) Throughout the year
8. How is Periwinkle plant propagated?
   a) Stem cutting b) Seed propagation
   c) Both a and b d) Neither a nor b
9. What is the fertilizer plan for optimal growth of Periwinkle?
   a) Balanced NPK ratio b) High nitrogen content
   c) High phosphorus content d) High potassium content
10. How often is irrigation done for Periwinkle plants?
    a) 2-3 times a month b) 4-5 times at 15-day intervals
    c) Daily d) Weekly

Short answer questions

1. Describe the botanical characteristics of Periwinkle, including its leaves, flowers, and roots.
2. Discuss the medicinal importance of Periwinkle, highlighting its anticancer properties and the alkaloids responsible for these properties.
3. Explain the ideal climate and soil conditions for cultivating Periwinkle, and describe the common practices used for its cultivation.
4. What are the different methods of propagation used for Periwinkle? Describe the advantages and disadvantages of each method.
5. Discuss the economic importance of Periwinkle, including its commercial cultivation, harvesting, and post-harvest management practices.

Answers for MCQ

1. a) Catharanthus roseus
2. a) Leaves
3. b) 100 cm
4. d) All of the above
5. a) Rosindin
6. a) CIMAP
7. d) Throughout the year
8. c) Both a and b
9. a) Balanced NPK ratio
10. b) 4-5 times at 15-day intervals

References

Bayanloo, E., Aelaei, M. and Khani, M.S., 2020. Catharanthus roseus L.(G. DON). Iranian Journal of Horticultural Science, 50(4), pp.993-1008.

Dovrat, A. and Goldschmidt, J., 1977, July. Cultivation aspects of Catharanthus roseus for roots. In I International Symposium on Spices and Medicinal plants 73 (pp. 263-268).

Mishra, J.N. and Verma, N.K., 2017. A brief study on Catharanthus roseus: A review. Intern J Res Pharmacy Pharmaceut Sci, 2(2), pp.20-23.

Paarakh, M.P., Swathi, S., Taj, T., Tejashwini, V. and Tejashwini, B., 2019. Catharanthus roseus Linn-a review. Acta Scientific Pharmaceutical Sciences, 3(10), pp.19-24.

Retna, A.M. and Ethalsha, P., 2013. A review of the taxonomy, ethnobotany, chemistry and pharmacology of Catharanthus roseus (Apocyanaceae). Int J Eng Res Technol, 2(10), pp.3899-912.

9

Sarpagandha

Scientific name: *Rauvolfia serpentina (L.) Benth. ex Kurz*

Family: Apocyanaceae

Rauvolfia serpentina, also spelled as Rauwolfia, is indeed a vital plant in traditional Indian medicine. It has been used in folk medicine for centuries to treat conditions like snake and insect bites, malaria, dysentery, and more. This plant is deeply rooted in Indian culture, mentioned in Hindu manuscripts as far back as 1000 BCE. It's also known by various names, including Indian snake root, devil pepper, serpentine wood, sarpagandha, and chandrika. Botanically, it belongs to the family Apocynaceae, with the genus Rauvolfia comprising 74 species. Unfortunately, *Rauvolfia serpentina* is listed as endangered due to over-exploitation and habitat loss, emphasizing the need for conservation and sustainable use to ensure its availability for future generations.

Origin and distribution

The distribution of *R. serpentina* is very wide, is occurrence is sporadic. The plant commonly grows scattered and close to each other. They are widely distributed in the Sub Himalayan tract from Himachal Pradesh to Sikkim and Bhutan, Eastern and Western Ghats, in some parts of central India. Beyond India the plant is distributed in Bangladesh, Malaysia, Thailand, Nepal, Sri Lanka, Indonesia, and Burma.

Botany

This perennial under-shrub stands upright, reaching heights of 75 cm to 1 m. Its bright green leaves are elliptical in shape and feature pointed tips. The plant's inflorescence is characterized by clusters of white or pink flowers.

The fruit is a drupe, while the root system is notable for its tuberous, branching structure. The root diameter ranges from 0.5 to 2.5 cm, extending 40-60 cm deep into the soil. A significant portion of the root, approximately 40-60%, is comprised of bark rich in alkaloids.

Climate and soil

A climate with a range of temperature from 500F to 1000F is suitable for their growth. They prefer an annual rainfall of about 100 inches through the South West monsoon. They grow well in hot humid climate, preferring partial shade in tropical or sub tropical belt and have the benefit of monsoon rains.

R. serpentine can grow in a variety of soils. Sandy alluvial loam, red lateric loam, and stiff dark loam are suitable for their growth. It can grow in clayey or sandy loam to laterites soils. Well drained, acidic soils with pH of 4.6-6.5 are good for their growth. They prefer soil rich in humus.

Chemical constituents

The main chemical components of *Rouvolfia* are alkaloids. The plant contains 40 types of alkaloids. Also it contains phytosterols, unsaturated alcohols, fatty acids and sugar as chemical constituents. Reserpine and Rescinnamine are alkaloids which have main therapeutical effect it *R.serpentine.* The plant contains indole alkaloids and iridoid glycoside, 7-epiloganin, which is a new sucrose derivative. Ajmaline and Ajmalicine are also present in the plant. the dried roots of *R.serpentine* shows the presence of new indole alcohol, N(b)-methyl ajmaline, N(b)-methyl iso ajmaline, 3-hydroxy sarpagine, yohimbinic acid, iso rouhimbinic acid.

Season

For nursery sowing, the optimal seasons are March-April or September-October. Transplanting can be done in May-June or November-December when the seedlings are 6-8 inches tall. Root cuttings are planted in spring, while stem cuttings are planted in June.

Land preparation

The land is prepared in April and May by deep ploughing and weathering. After pre-monsoon showers, 40 tonnes of farm yard manure (FYM) per hectare is added, followed by ploughing and harrowing. The land is then planked and beds are laid out.

Planting material and planting technique

Sarpagandha can be propagated through seeds, stem cuttings, or root cuttings. Seed propagation is the best method for commercial plantations. Seeds are sown in nursery beds, and seedlings are transplanted at a distance of 30cm within rows spaced 45cm apart.

Irrigation

Sarpagandha requires regular irrigation, especially in high temperatures and low rainfall. It prefers 15-20 irrigations at 20-day intervals in summer and 30-day intervals in winter.

Manures and fertilizer

For optimal growth and yield, Sarpagandha requires adequate nutrients. Organic manures like Farm Yard Manure (FYM) at 10-15 tonnes per hectare, Vermicompost at 2-3 tonnes per hectare, and Green Manure at 2-3 tonnes per hectare can be used. In addition, inorganic fertilizers such as NPK @ 100:50:50 kg per hectare can be applied. Micronutrients like Zinc Sulphate (20-30 kg per hectare), Borax (10-20 kg per hectare), and Copper Sulphate (10-20 kg per hectare) can also be used.

Weeding

The field must be kept weed-free, especially during the initial growth period. Weeding is done 2-3 times in the first year if Sarpagandha is the sole crop and 5-6 times if it's intercropped with other crops.

Plant protection

The plant is susceptible to diseases like leaf blight, bud rot, and leaf spot. Bio-pesticides prepared from neem, chitrakmool, and cow urine are used to prevent diseases and pests like pyralid caterpillars.

Harvesting

Sarpagandha roots are harvested after 18 months of planting. The ideal harvesting time coincides with the shedding of leaves during early autumn. At this stage, the roots contain a high concentration of total alkaloids. Harvesting involves digging up the roots, which can extend up to 40cm deep in the soil. Thin roots are also collected during harvesting.

Yield

The root yield of Sarpagandha varies from 1.5 to 2.5 tonnes per hectare of dry weight under irrigation. The yield is influenced by factors such as soil fertility, crop stand, and management practices.

Postharvest handling

After harvesting, the roots are cleaned, washed, and cut into 12-15 cm pieces for easy drying and storage. The dried roots contain 8-10% moisture and are stored in polythene-lined gunny bags in a cool, dry place. This helps protect the roots from mold and preserves their quality.

MCQ questions

1. What is the optimal duration for Sarpagandha cultivation to obtain maximum root yield?
   a) 12 months b) 18 months
   c) 24 months d) 36 months
2. Which of the following is NOT a suitable soil type for Sarpagandha cultivation?
   a) Sandy alluvial loam b) Red lateric loam
   c) Stiff dark loam d) Alkaline soil
3. What is the ideal pH range for Sarpagandha cultivation?
   a) 4.6-6.5 b) 6.5-7.5
   c) 7.5-8.5 d) 8.5-9.5
4. Which of the following is a major chemical constituent of Sarpagandha?
   a) Alkaloids b) Glycosides
   c) Flavonoids d) Terpenoids
5. What is the average root yield of Sarpagandha per hectare under irrigation?
   a) 1-1.5 tonnes b) 1.5-2.5 tonnes
   c) 2.5-3.5 tonnes d) 3.5-4.5 tonnes
6. When is the ideal time for harvesting Sarpagandha roots?
   a) Early summer b) Late summer
   c) Early autumn d) Late autumn
7. How deep can Sarpagandha roots extend into the soil?
   a) Up to 20cm b) Up to 30cm
   c) Up to 40cm d) Up to 50cm
8. What is the moisture content of dried Sarpagandha roots?
   a) 5-7% b) 8-10%
   c) 10-12% d) 12-15%
9. How are dried Sarpagandha roots typically stored?
   a) In polythene-lined gunny bags b) In jute bags
   c) In cardboard boxes d) In plastic containers
10. What is the purpose of storing Sarpagandha roots in a cool, dry place?
    a) To promote mold growth b) To prevent mold growth
    c) To enhance flavor d) To increase shelf life

Short answer questions

1. Explain soil and climate conditions for Rouvolfia serpentina
2. Give an account on the cultivation practices for Rouvolfia serpentina
3. Explain method of harvesting
4. Post harvesting technologies and value additions for Rouvolfia serpentina
5. Describe the chemical constituents in Rouvolfia serpentina

Answers for MCQ

1. b) 18 months
2. d) Alkaline soil
3. a) 4.6-6.5
4. a) Alkaloids
5. b) 1.5-2.5 tonnes
6. c) Early autumn
7. c) Up to 40cm
8. b) 8-10%
9. a) In polythene-lined gunny bags
10. b) To prevent mold growth

References

Bhattacharjee, T., Sen, S., Chakraborty, R., Maurya, P.K. and Chattopadhyay, A., 2020. Cultivation of medicinal plants: Special reference to important medicinal plants of India. Herbal medicine in India: Indigenous knowledge, practice, innovation and its value, pp.101-115.

Chauhan, P.S., Chaurasiya, R.K. and Chand, P., 2019. Chapter-6 Sarpagandha: An Overview. Chief Editor, 141.

Mishra, S.P., Padhiary, A.K. and Nandi, A., Chapter-4 Production Technology, Post-Harvest Management and Value Addition of Sarpagandha. Advances in Horticulture, 39, p.53.

Shitiz, K. and Gupta, S.P., 2021. Rauwolfia serpentina. Himalayan Medicinal Plants, pp.111-149.

Wahurwagh, A., 2021. Sarpagandha (Rauwolfia Serpentina L.) (Doctoral Dissertation, Dr. Panjabrao Deshmukh Krishi Vidyapeeth).

10

Sweet Flag

Scientific name: ***Acorus calamus L.***

Family: Acoraceae

Acorus calamus, commonly known as Sweet Flag, is a medicinal plant with a long history of therapeutic use. Various names in Hindi, Sanskrit, and other languages know it. The plant has a distinctive lemon-like scent in its leaves and a pleasant aroma in its roots. Sweet Flag is highly valued for its essential oil used in the perfume industry. Unfortunately, the plant is now classified as an endangered species due to over-exploitation.

Origin and distribution

Acorus calamus, commonly known as Sweet Flag, is native to northern latitude countries worldwide. It is widely dispersed across the USA and can be found growing wild or cultivated in India and Sri Lanka up to 1800 meters.

Botany

Sweet Flag is a perennial, semi-aquatic herb that exhibits a distinctive morphology. The rhizome, which serves as the plant's stem, is cylindrical in shape, measuring 19-25 mm in diameter and 10 cm in length. The exterior of the rhizome is light brown in color, while the interior is white and spongy. The rhizome is also highly aromatic, emitting a sweet, pungent scent when bruised. It is a creeping, highly branched structure that allows the plant to spread rapidly.

The leaves of Sweet Flag are thick, erect, and sword-shaped, resembling those of the iris. They are bright green in color, with a waxy texture and a prominent midrib. The leaves are arranged in a basal rosette pattern, with the oldest leaves situated at the base of the plant. When bruised, the leaves emit a strong, sweet scent that is reminiscent of citrus.

The inflorescence of Sweet Flag is a cylindrical spike that bears small, yellow flowers. The spike is typically 5-10 cm in length and is situated at the apex of the plant. The flowers are densely arranged along the spike, with each flower measuring approximately 3-5 mm in diameter. The flowers are bisexual, with three sepals and three petals that are fused together to form a small, tubular structure.

The fruit of Sweet Flag is a small, berry-like structure that contains several seeds. However, fruiting is a rare occurrence in Sweet Flag, as the plant typically reproduces vegetatively through its rhizome.

Climate and soil

Sweet Flag is a hardy plant that thrives in tropical to sub-tropical climates. It requires ample sunshine during growth and drying phases. The ideal temperature range for cultivation is between 10°C to 38°C, with annual rainfall between 70 and 250 cm. The plant can grow in various soil types, from loamy plains to sandy coastal soils.

Varieties

Notable varieties of Sweet Flag include CIM-Balya, released from CSIR CIMAP, and Swarna Swara, released from YSRHU, Andrapradesh.

Season

The ideal time for planting Sweet Flag is in March-April, with land preparation beginning before the onset of monsoon.

Land preparation

To prepare the land for Sweet Flag cultivation, plough the field twice or thrice before the rains. Create a fine tilth by watering the field and mixing in 1 ton of FYM and 1 ton of green leaf manure.

Planting material and planting technique

Propagation of Sweet Flag is primarily done through rhizomes. Cut the rhizomes into smaller pieces, sprout them, and plant them at a depth of 4 cm, with a spacing of 30 x 30 cm between plants.

Irrigation

During the rainy season, irrigate the crop if the rain stops for more than 7 days, maintaining at least 5 cm of water in the field. In the summer season, irrigate every 2-3 days, depending on the soil's water-holding capacity.

Manure and fertilizer

Apply compost/FYM at 15 t per hectare, along with phosphorus and potassium. One-third of nitrogen, 50 kg of phosphorus, and 25 kg of potassium are required as basal dose. Apply the second dose of nitrogen after one month of planting, and the third dose after two months.

Plant protection

Slug damage: Spray Neem oil solution and apply slug control measures.

Mealy bugs: Spray Neem oil solution and apply insecticidal soap.

Leaf spot: Spray Neem oil solution and apply fungicidal measures.

Harvest

Sweet Flag is ready for harvest after 6-8 months, when the lower leaves turn yellow and dry. Partially dry the field, leaving sufficient moisture for uprooting the plant.

Yield

The average yield of Sweet Flag is approximately 4.22 t of dry rhizomes or 10 t of fresh rhizomes per hectare.

Post harvest operations

Clean the uprooted rhizome, wash it with water, and cut it into 5-7.5 cm lengths. Remove fibrous roots, air-dry the rhizomes, and beat and rub them 2-3 times. Pack the dried rhizomes for transportation and process them into extract, oil, powder, and other useful products.

Drying

Dry the cut rhizomes by spreading them under shade to preserve the oil content.

MCQ questions

1. What is the scientific name of Sweet Flag?
   a) *Acorus calamus* b) *Acorus americanus*
   c) *Acorus aromaticus* d) *Acorus officinalis*
2. Which of the following is a common name for Sweet Flag in Hindi?
   a) Bach b) Gorbach
   c) Vacha d) All of the above
3. What is the ideal temperature range for cultivating Sweet Flag?
   a) 10°C to 20°C b) 10°C to 38°C
   c) 20°C to 30°C d) 30°C to 40°C
4. How often should Sweet Flag be irrigated during the summer season?
   a) Every day b) Every 2-3 days
   c) Every week d) Every fortnight

5. What is the average yield of Sweet Flag per hectare?
   a) 2.22 t of dry rhizomes
   b) 4.22 t of dry rhizomes
   c) 6.22 t of dry rhizomes
   d) 8.22 t of dry rhizomes
6. What is the primary method of propagation for Sweet Flag?
   a) Seeds
   b) Rhizomes
   c) Stem cuttings
   d) Leaf cuttings
7. What is the name of the variety of Sweet Flag released from CSIR CIMAP?
   a) CIM-Balya
   b) Swarna Swara
   c) Acorus calamus
   d) Vacha
8. How long does it take for Sweet Flag to mature?
   a) 3-4 months
   b) 6-8 months
   c) 9-10 months
   d) 12 months
9. What is the purpose of drying Sweet Flag rhizomes under shade?
   a) To preserve the oil content
   b) To increase the yield
   c) To improve the flavor
   d) To reduce the weight
10. What is the name of the variety of Sweet Flag released from YSHRU?
   a) Swarna Swara
   b) CIM-Balya
   c) Acorus calamus
   d) Vacha

Short answer questions

1. Describe the ideal climate and soil conditions for cultivating Sweet Flag.
2. What are the primary uses of Sweet Flag?
3. Explain the process of harvesting and drying Sweet Flag rhizomes.
4. Describe the method of propagation for Sweet Flag.
5. What are the common pests and diseases that affect Sweet Flag, and how are they controlled?

Answers for MCQ

1. a) Acorus calamus
2. d) All of the above
3. b) 10°C to 38°C
4. b) Every 2-3 days
5. b) 4.22 t of dry rhizomes

6. b) Rhizomes
7. a) CIM-Balya
8. b) 6-8 months
9. a) To preserve the oil content
10. a) Swarna Swara

References

Balakumbahan, R., Rajamani, K. and Kumanan, K., 2010. Acorus calamus: An overview. Journal of Medicinal Plants Research, 4(25), pp.2740-2745.

Imam, H., Riaz, Z., Azhar, M., Sofi, G. and Hussain, A., 2013. Sweet flag (Acorus calamus Linn.): An incredible medicinal herb. International Journal of Green Pharmacy (IJGP), 7(4).

Khwairakpam, A.D., Damayenti, Y.D., Deka, A., Monisha, J., Roy, N.K., Padmavathi, G. and Kunnumakkara, A.B., 2018. Acorus calamus: a bio-reserve of medicinal values. Journal of basic and clinical physiology and pharmacology, 29(2), pp.107-122.

Lokesh, G.B., 2004. Sweet flag (Acorus calamus) -Cultivation and Economics aspects.

Umamaheshwari, N. and Rekha, A., 2018. Sweet flag:(Acarus calamus)-An incredible medicinal herb. Journal of Pharmacognosy and Phytochemistry, 7(6), pp.15-22.

11

White Dill

Scientific name: Ammi majus L.

Family: Apiaceae

Ammi majus L., a member of the Apiaceae family, is a valuable medicinal plant. Its botanical name is derived from the Greek words "Ammi" and "majus," meaning "sand" and "larger," respectively. This plant has been used for centuries in traditional medicine, particularly for its antispasmodic and anti-inflammatory properties.

Origin and distribution

Ammi majus L. is native to Egypt and is now cultivated in various parts of the world, including India, Europe, and North Africa. It has been introduced to many countries for its medicinal and ornamental value.

Botany

This herbaceous annual plant grows up to a height of 0.75 to 1.15 meters. It has a round, erect, and solid stem with a tap root system. The large leaves are 5-8 cm long, alternate, and light green, with a compound, pinnately divided, and lanceolate shape.

The inflorescence is an umbel, axillary, and terminal in position, bearing white flowers. The calyx tube is adnate to bracts, with 5 teeth. The petals are 5 in number, epigynous, distinct, and bifid. There are 5 stamens, epigynous, and alternate with petals. The ovary is inferior, 2-celled, disk epigynous, 2-lobed, with a solitary ovule in each cell. The style has 2 branches, with a minute and capitulate stigma.

Flowering occurs after 3-4 months of seed sowing. The fruit is a pod, ribbed, ellipsoid, and greenish-brown in color, turning reddish-brown on maturity. It is ready within 30-35 days from blossoming. The seeds are flat, bearing thin wings, with a characteristic odor that becomes strong on crushing. They have an extremely pungent and slightly bitter taste.

Climate and soil

This plant thrives in moderate climates with mild winters and warm summers. It prefers well-drained, sandy loam to clay loam soils rich in organic matter. The ideal temperature for growth is between 27-32°C, and it requires adequate moisture, especially during the germination and seedling stages.

Chemical composition

The fruits of Ammi majus L. contain 1% glucoside, 0.45% tannin, 4.76% oleoresin, 3.2% acrid oil, 12.92% fixed oil, 13.83% proteins, and 22.4% cellulose. The major constituents are furanocoumarins, including xanthotoxins (methoxsalen, 8-methoxypsoralen, ammoidin, up to 1.15%), imperatorin (ammidin, up to 0.75%), and bergaptens (heraclin, majudin, 5-methoxypsoralen, up to 1.88%). Other compounds present include marmesin, isoimperatorin, heraclenin, and isopimpinellin.

Varieties

There are two main varieties of Ammi majus L.: Suttons and Monoica. These varieties differ in their growth habits, leaf morphology, and flowering patterns.

Season

The ideal time for planting Ammi majus L. is in September-October, when the weather is cool and moist. This allows for optimal germination and seedling growth.

Land preparation

The field is prepared by plowing, leveling, and making plots of convenient size. The soil is loosened to a depth of 20-25 cm to allow for proper root growth.

Planting material and planting technique

Ammi majus is propagated through seeds, which can be sown directly in the field or first raised in a nursery. The seeds are sown in rows 10 cm apart, and covered with a layer of rice-straw, wheat-straw, or dried grass. About 1.5-2.0 kg of seed is required for raising a crop in one hectare.

Irrigation

The irrigation frequency depends on climatic conditions, soil moisture status, and crop growth stage. The plant requires adequate moisture, especially during the germination and seedling stages. The field should be irrigated immediately after transplanting and thereafter at an interval of 7-10 days, depending on weather conditions.

Weeding

Regular weeding is necessary to prevent competition for space, light, moisture, and nutrients. Weeding can be done manually or mechanically, taking care not to damage the crop.

Manures and fertilizers

The plant responds well to nutrient application. A balanced fertilizer dose of 80-100 kg N, 100-120 kg P2O5, and 40 kg K2O per hectare is recommended for optimal growth.

Plant protection

Common pests affecting *Ammi majus* include aphids, slugs, and thrips. Diseases include Botrytis, damping off, and powdery mildew. Integrated pest management strategies, such as introducing natural predators, practicing good sanitation, and using organic pesticides, are recommended.

Harvesting

Ammi majus is a 5-7 month duration crop. The umbels are harvested manually at every 3-4 day interval to avoid seed shattering and wastage. The harvested produce is kept in a shady, well-ventilated place and thereafter threshing operation is carried out.

Yield

The seed yield varies depending on factors like variety, planting time, spacing, and harvesting stage. An average seed yield of 1000-1200 kg per hectare is achieved in well-managed fields.

MCQ questions

1. What is the scientific name of White Dill?
   a) *Ammi majus* L. b) *Apium graveolens*
   c) *Anethum graveolens* d) *Foeniculum vulgare*
2. Which family does *Ammi majus* L. belong to?
   a) Apiaceae b) Brassicaceae
   c) Solanaceae d) Lamiaceae
3. What is the ideal temperature for the growth of *Ammi majus* L.?
   a) 20-25°C b) 27-32°C
   c) 35-40°C d) 45-50°C
4. What is the primary use of *Ammi majus* L.?
   a) Food b) Medicine
   c) Ornamental d) Insecticide

5. Which of the following is a major constituent of *Ammi majus* L.?
   a) Alkaloids b) Glycosides
   c) Furanocoumarins d) Terpenes
6. What is the average seed yield of *Ammi majus* L. per hectare?
   a) 500-600 kg b) 1000-1200 kg
   c) 1500-1800 kg d) 2000-2500 kg
7. Which of the following is a common pest affecting *Ammi majus* L.?
   a) Aphids b) Whiteflies
   c) Thrips d) All of the above
8. What is the ideal time for planting *Ammi majus* L.?
   a) March-April b) September-October
   c) May-June d) November-December
9. Which of the following is a disease affecting *Ammi majus* L.?
   a) Powdery mildew b) Botrytis
   c) Damping off d) All of the above
10. What is the duration of the *Ammi majus* L. crop?
   a) 3-4 months b) 5-7 months
   c) 9-10 months d) 12 months

Short answer questions

1. Describe the chemical composition of Ammi majus L.
2. What are the ideal climatic conditions for the growth of Ammi majus L.?
3. Explain the process of harvesting Ammi majus L.
4. What are the common pests and diseases affecting Ammi majus L.?
5. Describe the nutritional value of Ammi majus L.

Answers for MCQ

1. a) Ammi majus L.
2. a) Apiaceae
3. b) 27-32°C
4. b) Medicine
5. c) Furanocoumarins
6. b) 1000-1200 kg
7. d) All of the above

8. b) September-October
9. d) All of the above
10. b) 5-7 months

References

Akbar, S. and Akbar, S., 2020. Ammi majus L. and A. visnaga (L.) Lam.(Apiaceae/ Umbelliferae). Handbook of 200 Medicinal Plants: A Comprehensive Review of Their Traditional Medical Uses and Scientific Justifications, pp.243-249.

Duke, J.A., 1988. Bishop's weed (Ammi majus L., Apiaceae). Economic Botany, 42(3), pp.442-445.

Hossain, M.A. and Al Touby, S., 2020. Ammi majus an endemic medicinal plant: a review of the medicinal uses, pharmacological and phytochemicals. Annual toxicology, 2, pp.9-14.

Janardhanan, M., 2004. Herb and spice essential oils. Discovery Publishing House.

Usmani, Q.I., Jahan, N., Aleem, M. and Hasan, S.A., 2021. Aatrilal (Ammi majus L.), an important drug of Unani system of medicine: A review. Journal of Ethnopharmacology, 276, p.114144.

12

Citronella

Scientific name: *Cymbopogon* spp.

Family: Poaceae

Citronella was first introduced in India in 1959 from Indonesia, specifically from Java Island, which is why it is also known as Java citronella. This fragrant grass, belonging to the Poaceae family, yields essential oils when steam-distilled. The resulting citronella oil (*Cymbopogon winterianus* Jowitt) is widely used globally in various industries, including flavoring, soap, perfumery, and cosmetics.

There are two main types of citronella: Ceylon and Java. The species *C. nardus* yields Ceylon-type oil, while *C. winterianus* yields Java-type oil. Java-type oil is preferred over Ceylon-type oil due to its higher citronellal content, ranging from 30-38% compared to 20-25% in Ceylon-type oil.

Origin and distribution

Citronella originated in tropical Asia, specifically in Indonesia (Java Island) and Sri Lanka. Today, it is cultivated in many tropical and subtropical regions worldwide. In India, citronella is grown in several states, including Maharashtra, Uttar Pradesh, and Madhya Pradesh. It is also cultivated in other parts of Southeast Asia, such as Malaysia, the Philippines, and Thailand. Citronella is also grown in Africa, Central and South America, and the Pacific Islands, where the warm and humid climate provides ideal conditions for its growth.

Botany

Citronella grass is a tropical, perennial grass that grows up to 1-2 meters in height. It features long, slender stems and flat, linear leaves that are typically 1-2 cm wide and 30-100 cm long. The plant has a fibrous root system with numerous underground stolons that produce new shoots, and its inflorescence is a panicle, typically 15-30 cm long, with numerous spikelets containing small, fragrant flowers.

Climate and soil

Citronella plants are adaptable to various soil conditions, but they thrive best in sandy loam soil rich in organic matter. The ideal pH range for citronella cultivation is between 5.8 and 8.0. However, heavy clay and sandy soils are not suitable for the plant's growth and are highly sensitive to waterlogging. Citronella requires ample moisture and sunlight to achieve maximum yields. High atmospheric humidity and evenly spaced rainfall of 200-250 cm positively impact plant development, oil yield, and quality. It is recommended that citronella be cultivated below 400 meters altitude, as growing it at higher elevations can restrict its growth and lead to lower yields. Additionally, citronella can tolerate unfavorable soil conditions, including moisture stress.

Chemical composition

The essential oil of Citronella is primarily citronellal, geraniol, and citronellol. In addition to these major constituents, Citronella oil also contains other compounds, including citronellyl acetate, L-limonene, ellemol, and various sesquiterpene alcohols.

Season

The ideal time for planting Java citronella is with the onset of monsoon. However, planting can also be done in July-August and February-March.

Land preparation

To prepare the land for citronella cultivation, the soil is ploughed deeply and then pulverized using crisscross harrowing. The field is then laid out into 6-meter side beds, with irrigation channels in between. Ridges and furrows are made at 60 cm intervals. Adding 20-25 tons per hectare of farm yard manure (FYM) or compost and mixing it into the soil during the final stages of tillage is also beneficial.

Planting material

Citronella can only be propagated vegetatively, as it does not produce viable seeds. One-year-old clumps are dug up and divided into slips, each containing 2-3 tillers. The fibrous roots and leaves are trimmed from the slips before planting. Approximately 50 slips can be obtained from a one-year-old clump.

Irrigation

Citronella requires adequate moisture to grow well and produce a good amount of leaves. In regions with annual rainfall of 200-250 cm, evenly spread throughout the year, and high humidity, supplemental irrigation is not necessary. However, in drier months, irrigation can be provided to increase yields. On average, 25-30 irrigations are required per year.

Manures and fertilizers

The recommended basal dose is 40 kg per hectare per year of phosphorus (P) and potassium (K). However, the most effective level of phosphorus has been found to be 60 kg per hectare. The application of fertilizers also improves oil quality.

Weeding and intercultural operations

Citronella grows slowly and is susceptible to weeds, especially during the first 60 days after planting. Effective weed control measures include hand weeding, mulching with spent grass (5 tons per hectare), close spacing (30 x 30 cm), and application of herbicides like atrazine (1.0 kg ai per hectare) and butachlor (1.0 kg ai per hectare).

Plant protection

Plant protection measures are crucial to prevent damage to plants. Among insects, termites are reported to cause the most damage and can be controlled by applying insecticides to the soil when planting. Leaf blight and sheath blight disease can be controlled by prophylactic spraying of fungicides at intervals of 10-15 days during the growth period.

Harvesting

Citronella is typically harvested when the plants are around 6-8 months old, just before the onset of flowering. The leaves and stems are cut near the base of the plant, leaving a small portion of the stem intact to allow for regrowth. Harvesting can be done mechanically or manually, depending on the scale of production.

Yield

The average yield of citronella oil is around 150-200 kg per hectare per year. However, yields can vary depending on factors such as climate, soil quality, and farming practices.

Post harvest handling

After harvesting, the citronella leaves and stems are dried to reduce the moisture content. This can be done through various methods, including air drying, sun drying, or using mechanical dryers. The dried material is then stored in a cool, dry place to preserve the oil quality.

MCQ questions

1. Where was citronella first introduced in India?
   a) Java Island, Indonesia b) Sri Lanka
   c) Malaysia d) Thailand
2. What is the primary use of citronella oil?
   a) Perfumery and cosmetics b) Flavoring and food industry
   c) Pharmaceuticals and medicine d) All of the above
3. Which type of citronella oil is preferred globally due to its higher citronellal content?
   a) Ceylon-type oil b) Java-type oil
   c) Indian-type oil d) Chinese-type oil
4. What is the ideal pH range for citronella cultivation?
   a) 5.0-6.0 b) 5.8-8.0
   c) 6.5-7.5 d) 7.0-8.5
5. How often should citronella be irrigated in regions with low rainfall?
   a) 10-15 irrigations per year b) 20-25 irrigations per year
   c) 25-30 irrigations per year d) 30-35 irrigations per year
6. What is the recommended basal dose of phosphorus and potassium per hectare per year?
   a) 20 kg P and 30 kg K b) 40 kg P and 40 kg K
   c) 60 kg P and 60 kg K d) 80 kg P and 80 kg K
7. Which insect is reported to cause the most damage to citronella plants?
   a) Termites b) Aphids
   c) Whiteflies d) Caterpillars
8. At what age are citronella plants typically harvested?
   a) 3-4 months b) 6-8 months
   c) 9-12 months d) 1-2 years
9. What is the average yield of citronella oil per hectare per year?
   a) 100-150 kg b) 150-200 kg
   c) 200-250 kg d) 250-300 kg
10. What is the purpose of drying citronella leaves and stems after harvesting?
    a) To reduce moisture content b) To increase oil quality
    c) To prevent spoilage d) All of the above

Short answer questions

1. Describe the origin and distribution of citronella.
2. What are the different types of citronella oil, and how do they differ in terms of citronellal content?
3. Explain the process of land preparation and planting for citronella cultivation.
4. What are the recommended manures and fertilizers for citronella cultivation, and how do they impact oil quality?
5. Describe the harvesting and post-harvest handling processes for citronella.

Answers for MCQ

1. a) Java Island, Indonesia
2. d) All of the above
3. b) Java-type oil
4. b) 5.8-8.0
5. c) 25-30 irrigations per year
6. b) 40 kg P and 40 kg K
7. a) Termites
8. b) 6-8 months
9. b) 150-200 kg
10. d) All of the above

References

Akhila, A., 2009. Essential oil-bearing grasses: the genus Cymbopogon. CRC press.

Blank, A.F., Costa, A.G., Arrigoni-Blank, M.D.F., Cavalcanti, S.C., Alves, P.B., Innecco, R., Ehlert, P.A. and Sousa, I.F.D., 2007. Influence of season, harvest time and drying on Java citronella (Cymbopogon winterianus Jowitt) volatile oil. Revista Brasileira de Farmacognosia, 17, pp.557-564.

Marulanda, V.A., Gutiérrez, C.D.B. and Alzate, C.A.C., 2017. Citronella Oil. In Green Pesticides Handbook (pp. 151-184). CRC Press.

Singh, K., Kothari, S.K., Singh, D.V., Singh, V.P. and Singh, P.P., 2000. Agronomic studies in Cymbopogons–a review. Journal of Spices and Aromatic Crops, 9(1), pp.13-22.

Toungos, M.D., 2019. Lemongrass (Cymbopogon, L. Spreng) valuable grass but underutilized in Northern Nigeria. International Journal of Innovative Food, Nutrition and Sustainable Agriculture, 7(2), pp.6-14.

13

Geranium

Scientific name: *Pelargonium graveolens* L. Herit

Family: Geraniaceae

Geranium, scientifically known as *Pelargonium graveolens* L. Herit, belongs to the Geraniaceae family. This aromatic plant is highly valued for its essential oil, which boasts an intense rose-like fragrance. Geraniol and citronellol are the primary constituents of this oil. There are approximately 600 species within the genus Pelargonium, many of which possess a pleasant odor, although only a few have attained commercial significance.

Types of Geranium

There are two primary types of geranium:

Algerian or Tunisian Type: Characterized by slender, erect plants with dark pink flowers. This variety contains 0.3% oil, with 57% 1-citronellol. It is commonly grown in the Nilgiris and is unsuitable for wet conditions.

Reunion or Bourbon Type: Produces more bushy growth with light-pink flowers. The oil has a higher 1-citronellol content (59.4%). This variety is grown in the Nilgiris and Anamalais and is more suitable for wet conditions.

Origin and distribution

Geranium is commercially cultivated in several countries, including France, Belgium, Spain, Morocco, Madagascar, Egypt, Reunion Island, Congo, China, India, and the former USSR countries. The global production of geranium oil is estimated to be 250-300 tons, while the annual demand exceeds 500 tons. In India, the first high-yielding *Pelargonium graveolens* plants were introduced from Reunion Island and planted in Yercaud by a French planter in the early 20th century. Since then, geranium has been cultivated commercially in high-altitude areas with mild climates. However, the crop also thrives in the South Indian plains. Commercial cultivation is mainly concentrated in the Nilgiris and Kodaikanal Hills of Tamil Nadu, around Bangalore in Karnataka, and in the high-altitude regions of Jammu and Kashmir.

Botany

This plant is a bushy, aromatic shrub characterized by its distinctive stem, which is cylindrical in shape, woody at the base, and covered in fine hairs (pubescent). The stem's color transitions from green in youth to brown with age.

The leaves of this plant are alternate, stipulate, and simple, featuring 5 primary lobes accompanied by secondary lobes. They are densely covered in fine hairs (pubescent) and emit a potent, aromatic fragrance.

The inflorescence is umbellate in arrangement and hairy. Each flower is bisexual and hypogenous, boasting a vibrant pink corolla. The floral structure includes 10 stamens with sub-equal filaments united at the base, accompanied by 7 anthers.

The ovary is hairy, superior, and comprises five fused carpels (pentacarpellary and syncarpous). A hairy style emerges from the ovary, eventually breaking up into five distinct stigmas.

Climate and soil

Geranium can thrive in temperate, subtropical, and tropical climates. The ideal temperature range for its growth is between 5°C to 23°C. Temperatures below 3°C or above 30°C can be detrimental to the plant. Warm winters and mild summers with well-distributed annual rainfall of 100-150 cm are ideal. Geranium can tolerate higher temperatures of up to 43°C in the plains when grown under irrigated conditions. In terms of soil requirements, geranium prefers well-drained, porous soil rich in organic matter. Red lateritic soils with a pH value of 5.5 to 7.0, rich in calcium, are suitable for its growth. Geranium is a shallow-rooted crop and can thrive in a variety of soils. Scented geraniums are hybrid plants commonly grown from cuttings, which can be taken at any time of the year.

Chemical composition

The essential oil of Pelargonium graveolens is primarily composed of citronellol (37.5%), geraniol (6.0%), and other compounds such as caryophyllene oxide, menthone, linalool, β-bourbonene, iso-menthone, geranyl formate, cis-rose oxide, geranyl tiglate, and 2-phenylethyl tiglate. Additionally, the oil contains citronellol and geraniol in a 1:1 ratio, along with citronellyl formate, guaia-6,9-diene, and isomenthone.

Varieties

Several varieties of geranium have been developed for cultivation in different regions. Some of the notable varieties include Hemanti, Bipuli, and Kunti, which were released by the CIMAP, Lucknow, for cultivation in the plains of North India. Other popular varieties include KKL-1, Kelkar, Ooty, and IIHR Sel-8.

Season

The ideal season for geranium cultivation varies depending on the region. Geranium can generally be cultivated throughout the year except during extreme weather conditions. In India, the best time for planting geranium is:

In the plains: September-October or February-March

In the hills: March-April or September-October

This allows the crop to take advantage of the favorable climate and soil conditions, producing optimal growth and oil.

Land preparation

land preparation for geranium cultivation typically begins with selecting a well-drained, fertile land with a suitable pH range of 5.5-7.0. The land is then ploughed to a depth of 20-25 cm to loosen the soil and remove weeds. After ploughing, the land is harrowed to break the clods and prepare a smooth seedbed. The land is then levelled to ensure even drainage and a uniform soil surface.

Planting materials and planting techniques

Geranium is easily propagated through cuttings, as seed setting is absent. Terminal cuttings (20 cm long, 8 nodes) are ideal for propagation, giving 80% rooting without treatment. Cuttings are planted in raised beds, closely spaced (8-10 cm), and watered regularly. Before planting, cut ends are dipped in 0.1% Benlate solution. Nursery care includes temporary shade, regular watering, and bi-weekly spraying with 0.2% Urea solution.

For field planting, about 30,000 cuttings are required per hectare. Land preparation involves ploughing, ridging, and furrowing. Cuttings are planted at 60 cm x 60 cm spacing, irrigated immediately, and watered alternately for 10-15 days. Irrigation schedules are adjusted seasonally. Geranium tolerates short droughts but must avoid waterlogging.

Manures and fertilizers

Geranium responds well to the application of major and micro-nutrients. The recommended fertilizer dose includes 15-20 tons of well-decomposed FYM per hectare, along with 35 kg N, 35 kg P2O5, and 35 kg K2O per hectare through urea, super phosphate, and muriate of potash. A second dose of 35 kg N per hectare is applied two months after the first application. Additional doses of nitrogen, zinc sulphate, boron, copper, and molybdenum are applied in split doses after each harvest to increase herbage yield and oil production.

Plant protection

Plant protection measures are essential to prevent damage to plants. In terms of insects, caterpillars can cause holes in leaves and can be controlled by systemic insecticides. Whitefly can be a problem on regal pelargoniums, particularly in warm weather. Greenfly can also damage plants, distort leaves, and spread quickly. Sciarid flies, small black flies that damage roots, can be controlled by correct watering and using Jeyes Fluid.

Diseases can also affect plants. Black root rot, caused by *Thielaviopsis basicola*, can be controlled by fungicides. Damping-off is a fungal attack on seedlings, which can be controlled by using fungicide-treated seeds and avoiding soil drenching. Pelargonium rust affects zonal varieties and can be controlled by removing affected leaves and spraying fungicides. Oedema is caused by erratic watering and can be prevented by keeping roots moist. Finally, grey mould, caused by botrytis, can be controlled by removing damaged leaves and flowers, and providing adequate ventilation.

Harvesting

Geranium is typically harvested 4 months after transplanting, when the leaves turn light green and the odor changes from lemon-like to rose-like. Harvesting requires careful observation and experience. The crop is cut using a sharp sickle to minimize damage and sent for distillation immediately. After each harvest, the plant is hoed, fertilized, and irrigated according to schedule, allowing it to produce fresh shoots and reach the next harvesting stage in 4 months. This process can be repeated for 3-6 years, yielding a total of 3 harvests. Cultivation under polyhouse conditions can reduce the harvest time by 21 days.

Yield

The quality and yield of geranium oil depend on timely harvesting and maintaining a good plant population. A minimum of 25,000 plants per hectare can yield 15 kg of oil, with an oil recovery rate of 0.08-0.15%. Polyhouse cultivation can increase herb and oil yields by up to 53%.

Distillation of oil

Freshly harvested geranium terminals are used for oil distillation. The process involves stacking plant material near stills for 12-24 hours to facilitate fermentation and glycoside splitting. The oil is then extracted using a simple distillation method, where steam generated in a separate boiler is passed through the plant material. The condensed steam vapors and oil are then passed through a condenser with running cold water. The oil is separated from the water using the differential density method and clarified by filtering with activated carbon.

MCQ questions

1. What is the scientific name of the geranium plant?

   a) *Pelargonium graveolens* b) *Geranium graveolens*

   c) *Pelargonium roseum* d) *Geranium roseum*

2. Which family does the geranium plant belong to?

   a) Geraniaceae b) Rosaceae

   c) Lamiaceae d) Poaceae

3. What is the primary constituent of geranium essential oil?

   a) Citronellol b) Geraniol

   c) Linalool d) Caryophyllene oxide

4. How many species are there within the genus Pelargonium?

   a) Approximately 100 b) Approximately 300

   c) Approximately 600 d) Approximately 1000

5. What is the ideal temperature range for geranium growth?

   a) 0°C to 15°C b) 5°C to 23°C

   c) 10°C to 30°C d) 15°C to 35°C

6. How often can geranium be harvested in a year?

   a) 2-3 times b) 3-4 times

   c) 4-5 times d) 5-6 times

7. What is the recommended fertilizer dose for geranium cultivation?

   a) 10-15 tons of FYM per hectare

   b) 15-20 tons of FYM per hectare

   c) 20-25 tons of FYM per hectare

   d) 25-30 tons of FYM per hectare

8. Which insect can cause holes in geranium leaves?

   a) Caterpillars b) Whiteflies

   c) Greenflies d) Sciarid flies

9. What is the purpose of stacking plant material near stills for 12-24 hours before oil distillation?
   a) To facilitate fermentation and glycoside splitting
   b) To increase oil yield
   c) To improve oil quality
   d) To reduce oil recovery rate
10. What is the oil recovery rate of geranium oil?
   a) 0.05-0.10%
   b) 0.08-0.15%
   c) 0.10-0.20%
   d) 0.15-0.25%

Short answer questions

1. Describe the origin and distribution of geranium.
2. What are the different types of geranium, and how do they differ in terms of oil composition?
3. Explain the process of land preparation and planting for geranium cultivation.
4. What are the recommended manures and fertilizers for geranium cultivation, and how do they impact oil yield and quality?
5. Describe the harvesting and distillation processes for geranium oil.

Answers for MCQ

1. a) Pelargonium graveolens
2. a) Geraniaceae
3. a) Citronellol
4. c) Approximately 600
5. b) 5°C to 23°C
6. b) 3-4 times
7. b) 15-20 tons of FYM per hectare
8. a) Caterpillars
9. a) To facilitate fermentation and glycoside splitting
10. b) 0.08-0.15%

References

Babu, K.G. and Kaul, V.K., 2005. Variation in essential oil composition of rose-scented geranium (Pelargonium sp.) distilled by different distillation techniques. Flavour and fragrance journal, 20(2), pp.222-231.

Lis-Balchin, M. ed., 2002. Geranium and Pelargonium: History of Nomenclature, Usage and Cultivation. CRC Press.

Rajeswara Rao, B.R., Sastry, K.P., Prakasa Rao, E.V. and Ramesh, S.I., 1990. Variation in yields and quality of geranium (Pelargonium graveolens L'Hér. ex Aiton) under varied climatic and fertility conditions. Journal of Essential Oil Research, 2(2), pp.73-79.

Ram, M., Ram, D. and Roy, S.K., 2003. Influence of an organic mulching on fertilizer nitrogen use efficiency and herb and essential oil yields in geranium (Pelargonium graveolens). Bioresource technology, 87(3), pp.273-278.

Rezaei Nejad, A. and Ismaili, A., 2014. Changes in growth, essential oil yield and composition of geranium (Pelargonium graveolens L.) as affected by growing media. Journal of the Science of Food and Agriculture, 94(5), pp.905-910.

14

Holy Basil

Scientific name: *Ocimum sanctum L.*

Family: Lamiaceae

The 'Sacred basil' or 'Holy basil', *Ocimum sanctum Linn.* a biennial shrub belonging to the family Lamiaceae, is commonly cultivated in gardens. The Hindus of India worship the species and is traditionally grown in courtyards and temples. The aromatic plants belonging to genus Ocimum is popularly known by the name Basil. Basil was derived from Greek word "Basilica" which means royal plant. Among the Ocimum genus *Ocimum basilicum* is variously known as Sweet basil, French basil or Common basil. *Ocimum sanctum* is known as sacred basil or Holy basil which is a very sacred plant according to Hindu belief.

Origin and distribution

Ocimum Sanctum has broad distributions, covering the entire Indian subcontinent, ascending up to 1,800 m in the Himalayas and as far as the Andaman and Nicobar Islands. This plant occupies a wide range of habitats.

Botany

Botanically, *Ocimum sanctum* is an erect, herbaceous, and softly hairy plant that exhibits extensive branching. It typically grows to a height of 30-75 cm. The leaves are entire, serrate, and pubescent on both sides, while the flowers are characterized by their purplish or crimson hue, arranged in racemes. The fruits of *Ocimum sanctum* are sub-globose or broadly ellipsoid in shape, slightly compressed, nearly smooth, and exhibit a pale brown or reddish coloration with small black markings. It is a biennial or triennial shrub.

Climate and soil

Sacred basil thrives well on a wide range of soils. Rich loam, poor laterite, saline and alkaline to moderately acidic soils are also well suited for its cultivation. Well drained soil helps in better vegetative growth. Water logged conditions can cause root-rot and results in stunted growth.

Chemical composition

The leaf volatile oil contains eugenol (1-hydroxy-2-methoxy-4 allylbenzene), euginal (also called eugenic acid), urosolic acid (2,3,4,5,6,6a,7,8,8a, 10,11,12,13,14b-tetradecahydro-1H-picene-4a carboxylic acid), carvacrol (5-isopropyl-2-methylphenol), linalool (3, 7-dimethylocta-1, 6-dien-3-ol), limatrol, caryophyllene (4,11,11-trimethyl-8-methylene-bicyclo[7.2.0]undec 4-ene), methyl carvicol (also called Estragol: 1-allyl-4-methoxybenzene) while the seed volatile oil have fatty acids and sitosterol; in addition, the seed mucilage contains some levels of sugars and the anthocyans are present in green leaves.

Season

The nursery can be raised in the third week of February and transplanting is generally done in the middle of April.

Land preparation

The land is brought to fine tilth and laid out into plots of convenient sizes. It is preferable to add 15 t/ha of farm yard manure and recommended fertilizers as basal dose during the preparation of land and should be mixed well in the soil.

Planting material and planting technique

Tulsi is propagated through seeds. Seeds will get deteriorated over generations, due to its high cross pollination. Hence, for fresh plantings, the growers have to take fresh seeds from the pedigree stock.

Preparation of nursery

Raised seed beds of 15 × 4 × 9 ft size should be thoroughly prepared and well manures by the addition of farm yard manure 10 kg per bed. About 200-300 g seeds are enough to raise the seedlings for transplanting in one hectare of land.

Transplanting

Seedlings of six weeks old and having 4-5 leaves are transplanted at a spacing of 40 × 40 cm

Irrigation

Regular irrigation or rain is definitely required by the plants throughout the entire growing period. Irrigation should be provided through sprinklers or drip irrigation system.

Manure and fertilizers

To maintain soil fertility, it is essential to replenish the soil regularly, as Tulsi is cultivated for its herbage. Apply 10 tons of farmyard manure (FYM) or compost per hectare before planting, ensuring that the FYM/compost is well-decomposed. Avoid using compost made from city waste, human excreta, and fresh manure for plant nutrition.

The recommended fertilizer dose for Tulsi cultivation is: 120 kg of nitrogen (N): 60 kg of phosphorus (P2O5): 60 kg of potassium (K2O) per hectare

Apply half the dose of N and the entire dose of P2O5 and K2O as a basal dose. Split the remaining N into two doses, applying them after the first and second cuttings.

Intercultural operation

Weeds have to be managed before they start competing with the main crop for nutrients and light. First weeding is done one month after planting and the second 4 weeks later.

Plant protection

Tulsi is susceptible to a few insect pests and diseases. Insect pests include leaf rollers, which fold and web leaves together, and the Tulsi lace wing, which feeds on leaves and stems, causing curling and drying of the plant. This can be controlled by spraying insecticides.

Diseases affecting Tulsi include powdery mildew, seedling blight, and root rot. These can be managed by improving phyto-sanitary measures and using fungicides.

Harvesting

Care should be taken while harvesting Tulsi to avoid any type of contamination. Clean all the surfaces that comes into contact with the plant during and after harvest. The crop is to be harvested at full bloom stage to obtain maximum essential oil yield and better quality oil.

Processing

After harvesting, the produce may be allowed to wilt in the field for 4-5 hours to reduce moisture and bulkiness. However, delaying beyond 6-8 hours may impact oil quality and yield. Steam distillation is the preferred method for extracting essential oil.

Distillation and oil processing

The distillation unit should be clean, rust-free, and odor-free. The obtained oil is decanted, filtered, and treated with anhydrous sodium sulphate or common salt to remove moisture. The oil is stored in sealed, amber-colored glass bottles or containers made of stainless steel, galvanized tanks, or aluminum containers in a cool, dry place.

Chemical composition of sacred basil oil

The essential oil extracted from Sacred Basil leaves is bright yellow, with a pleasant aroma and a note of clove oil. The plant contains phenols, aldehydes, tannins, saponin, and fats. The essential oil components include:

Eugenol (71%), Eugenol methyl ether (20%), Carvacrol (3%). Minor portions of nerol, caryophyllene, selinene, α-pinene, ß-pinene, camphor, cineole, and linalool.

MCQ questions

1. What is the botanical name of Sacred Basil?
   a) *Ocimum basilicum*
   b) *Ocimum sanctum*
   c) *Ocimum americanum*
   d) *Ocimum kilimandscharicum*
2. Which of the following is NOT a suitable climate for Sacred Basil cultivation?
   a) Temperate b) Tropical
   c) Subtropical d) Arctic
3. What is the ideal time for sowing Sacred Basil seeds?
   a) First week of January b) Third week of February
   c) First week of April d) Third week of May
4. What is the spacing recommended for transplanting Sacred Basil seedlings?
   a) 20 × 20 cm b) 30 × 30 cm
   c) 40 × 40 cm d) 50 × 50 cm
5. What is the primary component of Sacred Basil essential oil?
   a) Eugenol b) Eugenol methyl ether
   c) Carvacrol d) Linalool
6. How many irrigations are required for Sacred Basil cultivation in a year?
   a) 8-10 b) 12-15
   c) 18-20 d) 22-25
7. What is the recommended fertilizer dose for Sacred Basil cultivation?
   a) 60 kg N, 30 kg P2O5, and K2O per hectare
   b) 120 kg N, 60 kg P2O5, and K2O per hectare
   c) 180 kg N, 90 kg P2O5, and K2O per hectare
   d) 240 kg N, 120 kg P2O5, and K2O per hectare

8. At what stage is Sacred Basil harvested to obtain maximum essential oil yield and better quality oil?

   a) Flowering stage b) Full bloom stage
   c) Fruiting stage d) Mature stage

9. What is the recommended method for extracting essential oil from Sacred Basil leaves?

   a) Steam distillation b) Hydro distillation
   c) Solvent extraction d) Cold pressing

10. How many days after planting is the first harvest of Sacred Basil obtained?

    a) 60-70 days b) 80-90 days
    c) 90-95 days d) 100-105 days

Short answer questions

1. Describe the origin, distribution, and cultural significance of Ocimum sanctum (Sacred Basil) in India.
2. What are the ideal climate and soil conditions for cultivating Sacred Basil? How does the plant adapt to different soil types?
3. Explain the process of land preparation, planting, and irrigation for Sacred Basil cultivation.
4. Describe the chemical composition of Sacred Basil essential oil, including its major and minor constituents.
5. Outline the harvesting, processing, and distillation procedures for obtaining high-quality Sacred Basil essential oil.

Answers for MCQ

1. b) Ocimum sanctum
2. d) Arctic
3. b) Third week of February
4. c) 40 × 40 cm
5. a) Eugenol
6. a) 8-10
7. b) 120 kg N, 60 kg P2O5, and K2O per hectare
8. b) Full bloom stage
9. a) Steam distillation
10. d) 100-105 days

References

Abeywardhana, K.W., Abeysinghe, D.C., Dharmadasa, R.M. and Aththanayake, A.M.L., 2014. Determination of optimum maturity stage for Ocimum sanctum L. grown under different growing systems in terms of therapeutically active secondary metabolites. World Journal of Agricultural Research, 2(4), pp.159-162.

Baseer, M. and Jain, K., 2016. Review of Botany, Phytochemistry, Pharmacology, Contemporary applications and Toxicology of Ocimum sanctum. International Journal of Pharmacy & Life Sciences, 7(2).

Cohen, M.M., 2014. Tulsi-Ocimum sanctum: A herb for all reasons. Journal of Ayurveda and integrative medicine, 5(4), p.251.

Kumar, R., Saha, P., Lokare, P., Datta, K., Selvakumar, P. and Chourasia, A., 2022. A systemic review of Ocimum sanctum (Tulsi): Morphological characteristics, phytoconstituents and therapeutic applications. International Journal for Research in Applied Sciences and Biotechnology, 9(2), pp.221-226.

Wang, M., Cantrell, C.L., Mathews, S.T., Paudel, P., Lee, J. and Mentreddy, S.R., 2022. Agronomy, chemical analysis, and antidiabetic activity of basil (Ocimum species). ACS Food Science & Technology, 2(8), pp.1243-1256.

15

Lavender

Scientific name: ***Lavandula angustifolia Mill.***

Family: Lamiaceae

Lavender is a small genus of perennial aromatic herbs, semi-shrubs, or shrubs. It comprises approximately 28 species, with three species being extensively utilized for extracting essential oils:

True Lavender (*Lavandula angustifolia*): One of the most important essential oils used in the perfumery industry.

Spike Lavender (*Lavandula latifolia*): Yields inferior oil, less fragrant than true lavender and rosemary.

Lavandin (*Lavandula hybrida*): is a hybrid of true lavender and spike lavender, possessing characteristics of both parents. The essential oil extracted from Lavandin combines the sweet, floral fragrance of true lavender with the camphoraceous harshness of spike lavender. Although Lavandin oil has a unique fragrance profile, it is considered inferior to true lavender oil in terms of quality and finesse.

Origin and distribution

Lavender originates from the Mediterranean basin, typically thriving in rocky, calcareous areas. Its distribution spans North Africa, the Mediterranean, Europe, and Western India. Lavender has been cultivated since ancient times, with the Greeks and Romans being notable cultivators. The name "lavender" is derived from the Latin verb "lavare," meaning "to wash" or "to bathe."

Botany

Lavender is a perennial, bushy shrub that grows 0.3 to 1.2 meters high, characterized by its compact, rounded growth form and aromatic, evergreen leaves that are opposite and up to 5 cm long. It produces fragrant, interrupted spike flowers in summer, with the flowering tops and leaves being used for essential oil distillation, although oil from the flowering tops is considered superior.

Climate and soil

Lavender is a hardy plant that can tolerate moderate frost and drought. However, spike lavender is sensitive to frost. All lavender varieties are sensitive to high humidity, and high summer temperatures can adversely affect oil quality.

In its natural habitat, true lavender grows at elevations up to 1,700 meters above sea level, while spike lavender is found in lower regions, typically between 200 to 700 meters above sea level. Lavandin is commonly found at heights of 700 to 1,000 meters above sea level. Oil yields tend to increase with altitude as plants flower more abundantly in cooler conditions.

Lavender is adaptable to various climatic zones, from cold to subtropical. Different varieties should be tested to determine which ones grow best in each microclimate. Lavender can thrive with an annual rainfall range of 300 to 1,400 mm per year. Allowing the soil to dry well between irrigations and avoiding over-irrigation is essential.

Lavender requires well-drained, light, sandy, or sandy loam soils in full sun. Low-fertility soils are still suitable, but the ideal soil pH should be between 5.8 and 8.3. Lavenders prefer alkaline soils; excessively moist soils can lead to poor plant growth, diseases, or even plant death.

Chemical composition

The phytochemical composition of lavender oil varies across different species, primarily consisting of monoterpeneoid and sesquiterpeneoid alcohols. The main constituents of lavender oil are linalool (20-35%) and linalyl acetate (30-55%), accompanied by moderate levels of lavandulyl acetate, terpinen-4-ol, lavandulol, 1,8-cineole, camphor, limonene, and tannins. Notably, lavender oil typically comprises over 100 compounds, although many of these are present in negligible concentrations.

Season

Lavender can be planted in autumn or spring, depending on the climate. In mild climates, autumn planting is best, while spring planting is recommended in areas with cold winters. Harvesting of lavender for essential oil should be undertaken when the flowers are well-developed and the lower half is starting to open.

Planting materials and planting techniques

Lavender can be propagated using seeds, cuttings, layering, tissue culture, or division of roots. Cuttings should be taken from strong and healthy plants, and rooting hormones can be used to encourage rooting. Planting density and spacing vary depending on the variety and climate. Lavender is normally planted in row widths of 1 to 2 m apart, with 30 to 60 cm spacing between the plants.

Irrigation

Irrigation is necessary for the first two years after planting, until the crop is established. Drip irrigation is recommended, as it reduces disease problems and weed growth. Overhead irrigation should be avoided, as it can increase disease problems.

Weeding and intercultural operations

Weeding can be done manually or mechanically, taking care not to damage the roots. Mulching can also help reduce weed incidence and retain soil moisture. Plant density and quick formation of a canopy can also help suppress weeds. Cover-cropping practices with plants that inhibit weed growth are also advised.

Manures and fertilisers

Lavender requires low levels of fertilization. Excessive nitrogen can decrease oil quality and promote weed growth. A balanced fertilizer with a pH between 6.0 and 7.0 is recommended. Periodic liming may be necessary to maintain the soil pH.

Pruning

Prune flower buds off lavender plants in the first two years to promote healthy growth and development. This helps establish a strong plant framework. After the harvesting season, prune lavender plants in the autumn, as harvesting for oil typically leaves most stalks intact. When pruning, leave 2-3 leaf-bearing nodes on vigorous cultivars, and prune less severely for slower-growing cultivars. Specialized trimmers can be used to mechanize the pruning process.

Plant protection

No serious diseases have been reported on lavender crops. Lavender is a natural pest repellent, and pest occurrences are rare and insignificant.

Harvesting

Lavender flowers are typically harvested when they are in full bloom, usually in late summer or early fall. The flowers should be cut just above the node, leaving a small portion of stem intact. Harvesting should be done during fine weather, as rain can reduce oil quality.

Yield

The yield of lavender oil can vary depending on factors such as climate, soil quality, and variety. On average, 100 kg of lavender flowers can produce 1-2 kg of essential oil.

Post harvest handling

Lavender oil production involves several methods. Firstly, sorting and distillation are crucial steps. Distillation can significantly impact the oil's value, as high pressure or temperature can alter the fragrance molecule's structure. The yield of oil varies from season to season, depending on factors like the age of the bushes and weather conditions.

Solvent extraction is another method used to produce lavender and lavandin concretes. This process involves using solvents like toluene, hexane, and petroleum ether to extract the concretes from fresh plant material. The solvents are then evaporated, leaving behind a residue called concretes. These concretes are used in the perfumery industry, particularly in soap production. Further refinement involves mixing the concretes with ethanol to produce an absolute.

Dried lavender flowers are also a valuable product. After harvesting, the flowers are tied in bundles and dried in the shade. Some flowers are stripped from the spikes after drying and packed into boxes or cases lined with paper. Notably, 8-10 kg of fresh flowers are required to produce just 1 kg of dry flowers.

Extraction of essential oil

The extraction of lavender essential oil typically involves steam distillation of the herbage. The essential oil content varies among different varieties, ranging from 0.5% to 1.1%, with an average oil content of 0.8%.

Packaging and storage

Proper packaging and storage are crucial to preserving essential oils' quality and potency. To achieve this, store essential oils in dark, air-tight glass bottles, avoiding exposure to heat, heavy metals, or direct sunlight. Regularly check for deterioration by monitoring the oil's color and viscosity. It may be degraded if the oil becomes darker or more viscous than usual.

Essential oils can remain potent for 6 months to 2 years with proper care. Alternative storage vessels like fluorinated plastic, treated aluminum, or dark glass/ceramic containers can also be used. For value-added markets, ensure that packaging is clearly labeled, neat, and professional.

MCQ questions

1. What method is primarily used to extract lavender essential oil?

   a) Solvent extraction   b) Steam distillation

   c) Cold pressing   d) Enfleurage

2. Which industry does NOT commonly use lavender concretes?
   a) Perfumery b) Soap production
   c) Food flavoring d) Pharmaceuticals
3. What is the average essential oil content in lavender varieties?
   a) 0.5% b) 0.8%
   c) 1.1% d) 1.5%
4. How long can essential oils remain potent with proper care?
   a) 1-3 months b) 6 months to 2 years
   c) 2-5 years d) 5-10 years
5. What is the recommended soil pH for lavender cultivation?
   a) 5.5-6.5 b) 6.0-7.0
   c) 7.0-8.0 d) 8.0-9.0
6. Which lavender species is known for its high-quality essential oil?
   a) *Lavandula angustifolia* b) *Lavandula latifolia*
   c) *Lavandula hybrida*
7. Why are lavender plants pruned in the first two years?
   a) To promote flowering
   b) To increase oil production
   c) To develop a strong plant framework
   d) To reduce water consumption
8. How many kilograms of fresh lavender flowers are needed to produce 1 kilogram of dried flowers?
   a) 5-6 kg b) 8-10 kg
   c) 12-15 kg d) 20-25 kg
9. What advantage does drip irrigation offer for lavender cultivation?
   a) Increased water consumption
   b) Improved disease resistance
   c) Enhanced weed growth
   d) Reduced soil erosion and disease risk
10. At what temperature range can lavender plants tolerate moderate frost?
    a) -5°C to 0°C b) 0°C to 5°C
    c) 5°C to 10°C d) 10°C to 15°C

Short answer questions

1. Describe the different species of lavender and their uses, including True Lavender, Spike Lavender, and Lavandin.
2. What are the ideal climatic and soil conditions for lavender cultivation, and how do different varieties adapt to various environments?
3. Outline the process of lavender propagation, including the use of seeds, cuttings, layering, tissue culture, and division of roots.
4. Describe the harvesting and post-harvest handling procedures for lavender, including the importance of proper packaging and storage for essential oils.
5. Explain the process of extracting lavender essential oil, including steam distillation, solvent extraction, and the production of concretes and absolutes.

Answers for MCQ

1. b) Steam distillation
2. d) Pharmaceuticals
3. b) 0.8%
4. b) 6 months to 2 years
5. b) 6.0-7.0
6. a) Lavandula angustifolia
7. c) T develop a strong plant framework
8. b) 8-10 kg
9. d) Reduced soil erosion and disease risk
10. b) 0°C to 5°C

References

Audette, F.L., 1997. Lavandula: an historical and horticultural perspective (Master's thesis, The Ohio State University).

Basch, E., Foppa, I., Liebowitz, R., Nelson, J., Smith, M., Sollars, D. and Ulbricht, C., 2004. Lavender (Lavandula angustifolia miller). Journal of herbal pharmacotherapy, 4(2), pp.63-78.

Crișan, I., Ona, A., Vârban, D., Muntean, L., Vârban, R., Stoie, A., Mihăiescu, T. and Morea, A., 2023. Current trends for lavender (Lavandula angustifolia Mill.) crops and products with emphasis on essential oil quality. Plants, 12(2), p.357.

Lim, T.K., 2014. Lavandula angustifolia. In Edible Medicinal and Non Medicinal Plants: Volume 8, Flowers (pp. 156-185). Dordrecht: Springer Netherlands.

Salahudin, H., Kamal, S., Akhter, N., Bibi, I., Rehman, K., Akash, M.S.H. and Gohar, U.F., 2023. Lavender. In Essentials of Medicinal and Aromatic Crops (pp. 965-982). Cham: Springer International Publishing.

16

Mint

Scientific name: *Mentha* spp.

Family: Lamiaceae

Mint belongs to the genus Mentha and is part of the Lamiaceae family, including popular herbs like basil, sage, and rosemary. There are several commercially grown mint species, each with unique chemical compositions, aromas, and uses.

Origin and distribution

Mint originated in the Mediterranean region and spread globally through natural and artificial means. Japanese mint is widely cultivated in Brazil, Paraguay, China, and India, while peppermint is grown in the USA, Morocco, Argentina, and Australia.

Botany

Japanese mint (*Mentha arvensis*) is a perennial, ascending herb that typically grows to a height of 60-80 cm, with the potential to reach up to 100 cm under favorable conditions. This herb is primarily propagated through its stolons, which enable it to spread and establish new plants. The leaves of Japanese mint are lanceolate-oblong in shape, featuring sharp teeth along their edges, and are supported by small petioles approximately 5 mm in length. The leaf lamina itself measures between 5 to 15 cm in length. Notably, the lower surface of the leaves is densely covered with hairy growths of glandular trichomes. The plant produces an abundance of small, purplish flowers in axillary and terminal verticillasters. These flowers are characterized by a corolla measuring 4-5 mm in length and a calyx that is narrowly deltoid and acuminate, measuring 2-3 mm. Japanese mint is sterile and does not produce seeds, relying solely on vegetative means of propagation.

Climate and soil

Mint requires a temperate climate with partial shade to full sun. It thrives in moist, fertile soils with a pH between 6.0 and 7.5. Japanese mint can be grown in tropical and subtropical areas, while peppermint and spearmint prefer humid, temperate climates.

Varieties

Several mint varieties are cultivated, including:

- Japanese mint (Mentha arvensis)
- Peppermint (Mentha piperita)
- Spearmint (Mentha spicata)
- Bergamot mint (Mentha citrata)

Season and planting

Mint is typically planted in winter or early spring. The ideal time for planting is from December to March, depending on the region.

Land preparation

Mint requires well-ploughed, harrowed soil with a pH between 6.0 and 7.5. Organic manure like FYM can be added at the time of land preparation.

Panting material and technique

Mint is propagated through stolons or suckers. The best time to obtain stolons is December and January. The stolons are planted in shallow furrows, and the plot is irrigated immediately after planting.

Irrigation and weeding

Mint requires frequent irrigation, especially during the early stages of growth. Weeding and hoeing are necessary to control weed growth and promote healthy plant growth.

Manure and fertilizer

Mint requires high amounts of nitrogenous fertilizers to promote healthy growth. A balanced fertilizer application of NPK (80-120 kg/ha, 50 kg/ha, and 40 kg/ha, respectively) is recommended.

Plant protection

Pests can damage mint plants, including the hairy caterpillar, which eats the undersurface of leaves, and cutworms, which damage young plants at the collar region. Red pumpkin beetles feed on growing leaves and buds, while mint leaf rollers fold and feed on leaves. Regular spraying of insecticides can help control these pests.

Mint plants are also susceptible to diseases like stolon rot, which causes brown lesions on underground parts, and fusarium wilt, which turns leaves yellow and curly. Leaf blight causes loss of foliage during summer. To manage these diseases, practices like crop rotation, treatment of stolons, and application of fungicides can be effective.

Harvest and yield

Mint is typically harvested after 100-120 days of planting. Fresh herbs contain 0.4% oil, and a good crop can yield up to 48 t/ha of fresh herbs. The average yield of oil is 50-70 kg/ha.

Distillation of oil

Mint oil is obtained through steam distillation of the fresh herb. The distillation process involves removing stems from the dried material prior to distillation.

MCQ questions

1. Which of the following mint varieties is known for its high-quality oil and is widely cultivated?
   a) Japanese mint b) Peppermint
   c) Spearmint d) Bergamot mint
2. Which family does the mint plant belong to?
   a) Lamiaceae b) Apiaceae
   c) Brassicaceae d) Solanaceae
3. Where did mint originate from?
   a) Mediterranean region b) Tropical region
   c) Subtropical region d) Temperate region
4. What is the ideal pH range for mint cultivation?
   a) 5.5-6.5 b) 6.0-7.5
   c) 7.0-8.0 d) 8.0-9.0
5. Which mint variety is widely cultivated in Brazil, Paraguay, China, and India?
   a) Japanese mint b) Peppermint
   c) Spearmint d) Bergamot mint
6. What is the average yield of mint oil per hectare?
   a) 30-50 kg/ha b) 50-70 kg/ha
   c) 70-90 kg/ha d) 90-100 kg/ha
7. How is mint oil obtained?
   a) Solvent extraction b) Steam distillation
   c) Cold pressing d) Enfleurage

8. What is the purpose of adding organic manure like FYM during land preparation for mint cultivation?
   a) To improve soil fertility
   b) To control weeds
   c) To prevent pests
   d) To promote healthy plant growth
9. Which pest eats the undersurface of mint leaves?
   a) Hairy caterpillar
   b) Cutworm
   c) Red pumpkin beetle
   d) Mint leaf roller
10. What is the name of the disease that causes brown lesions on underground parts of mint plants?
    a) Stolon rot
    b) Fusarium wilt
    c) Leaf blight
    d) Root rot

Short answer questions

1. What are the different types of mint varieties, and what are their distinct characteristics?
2. Explain the ideal climate and soil conditions for mint cultivation.
3. Outline the process of mint propagation, including the use of stolons or suckers.
4. Describe the common pests and diseases that affect mint plants and their management practices.
5. Explain the process of mint oil distillation, including the importance of removing stems from the dried material prior to distillation.

Answers for MCQ

1. b) Peppermint
2. a) Lamiaceae
3. a) Mediterranean region
4. b) 6.0-7.5
5. a) Japanese mint
6. b) 50-70 kg/ha
7. b) Steam distillation
8. d) To promote healthy plant growth
9. a) Hairy caterpillar
10. a) Stolon rot

References

Gupta, S., Kumar, A., Gupta, A.K., Jnanesha, A.C., Talha, M., Srivastava, A. and Lal, R.K., 2023. Industrial mint crop revolution, new opportunities, and novel cultivation ambitions: A review. Ecological Genetics and Genomics, 27, p.100174.

Salehi, B., Stojanović-Radić, Z., Matejić, J., Sharopov, F., Antolak, H., Kręgiel, D., Sen, S., Sharifi-Rad, M., Acharya, K., Sharifi-Rad, R. and Martorell, M., 2018. Plants of genus Mentha: From farm to food factory. Plants, 7(3), p.70.

Hedayati, S., Tarahi, M., Baeghbali, V., Tahsiri, Z. and Hashempur, M.H., 2024. Mint (*Mentha* spp.) essential oil extraction: From conventional to emerging technologies. Phytochemistry Reviews, pp.1-22.

Yousefian, S., Esmaeili, F. and Lohrasebi, T., 2023. A Comprehensive Review of the Key Characteristics of the Genus Mentha, Natural Compounds and Biotechnological Approaches for the Production of Secondary Metabolites. Iranian Journal of Biotechnology, 21(4), p.e3605.

Taneja, S.C. and Chandra, S., 2012. Mint. In Handbook of herbs and spices (pp. 366-387). Woodhead Publishing.

17

Musk

Scientific name: *Abelmoschus moschatus Medik.*

Family: Malvaceae

*Abelmoschus moschatus*Medik., commonly known as ambrette, annual hibiscus, or musk mallow, is a tropical plant species belonging to the Malvaceae family. Native to India, Southeast Asia, and Africa, this herbaceous plant has been cultivated for centuries for its medicinal, culinary, and fragrant properties. It is an annual or biennial plant that grows up to 2 meters in height, with hairy, palmate leaves and showy, yellow flowers with a purple center. The plant's seeds, leaves, and flowers emit a strong, musky fragrance used in perfumery and traditional medicine. *Abelmoschus moschatus* is a warm-season crop that thrives in tropical and subtropical regions, requiring well-drained soil and full sun to partial shade. The plant has been used in traditional medicine for its anti-inflammatory, antibacterial, and antifungal properties, and its leaves and flowers are used as a vegetable and in salads. In contrast, the seeds are used as a spice. The plant's essential oil is also used in perfumes, cosmetics, and aromatherapy products, making it a valuable crop for small-scale farmers, providing income through the sale of seeds, leaves, and essential oil.

Origin and distribution

Abelmoschus moschatus, a tropical plant species, is native to India and widely cultivated in Southern China, Vietnam, Nepal, Tropical Asia, South East Asia, and parts of the Pacific. It is also found in the tropical regions of Africa, Australia, and the Americas.

Botany

*Abelmoschus moschatus*Medik., a member of the Malvaceae family, is a native Indian plant renowned for its aromatic and medicinal properties. This erect, hispid herbaceous trailing herb grows up to 1.5 meters tall, characterized by a long, slender taproot. Its leaves are alternate, rough, hairy, and heart-shaped, typically bearing 3 to 5 lobes and reaching lengths of up to 15 centimeters.

The plant's flowers closely resemble those of the hibiscus, commonly exhibiting a watermelon pink hue, although white or cream-colored variations are also observed. These flowers are ephemeral, lasting only a single day, with their blooming pattern contingent upon the timing of the wet season.

Seeds are enclosed within hairy capsules measuring up to 8 centimeters in length, characterized by their tough yet papery texture. Notably, these seeds possess a sweet, flowery, and heavy fragrance reminiscent of musk.

Climate and soil requirements

Abelmoschus moschatus thrives in humid tropical or subtropical climates, tolerating temperatures up to 45°C. It requires fertile loamy or sandy-loamy soil, with poor growth on clay, sandy, saline, or strongly alkaline soils. The ideal pH range for cultivation is between 6.0 and 7.0.

Land preparation and sowing

The land is prepared by ploughing and harrowing, followed by leveling and mixing farmyard manure. Seeds are sown in well-prepared fields, 1 cm deep, with a 1.5 kg/ha seed rate. The optimal sowing time is during the monsoon season when the soil is moist and the temperature is warm.

Irrigation, manures, and fertilizers

The crop requires 6-7 irrigations at 20-25 day intervals, with moisture essential during the flower bud opening stage. A dose of 40, 30, and 30 kg of N, P, and K is applied basally, followed by 40 kg each at 40 and 90 days after germination. Additionally, a foliar spray of micronutrients such as boron, copper, and zinc can be applied to promote healthy plant growth.

Plant protection

Abelmoschus moschatus is generally disease-free, but can be infected by Hibiscus Mosaic Virus, Anthracnose, Alternaria leaf spot, and Phytophthora leaf blight, especially in humid conditions.

Pests that can damage the crop include the Egyptian stem borer, pink bollworm, and cotton semi-looper, which feed on various parts of the plant during different stages of growth.

Weeding, harvesting, and yield

The crop should be kept weed-free, with two weeding cum hoeing recommended. Pods are picked at weekly intervals when three-fourths of them turn blackish-brown. On average, a seed yield of 1 tonne/ha is obtained. The seeds can be stored for up to 6 months in a cool, dry place.

Post-harvest handling

After shade drying, pods are threshed, and husks are removed by winnowing. Steam distillation of whole seeds yields ambrette seed oil, while distillation of ground seeds and hydrocarbon extraction produce ambrette seed concrete. Ambrette seed absolute is prepared from the seed concrete through neutralization, elimination of fatty acids, or steam distillation. The oil is used in perfumery, aromatherapy, and traditional medicine.

MCQ questions

1. What is the scientific name of the musk plant?
   a) *Abelmoschus moschatus* b) *Hibiscus sabdariffa*
   c) *Abelmoschus esculentus* d) *Malva sylvestris*
2. Which family does the musk plant belong to?
   a) Malvaceae b) Fabaceae
   c) Solanaceae d) Lamiaceae
3. What is the ideal temperature range for cultivating musk?
   a) 20-30°C b) 30-40°C
   c) 40-45°C d) 45-50°C
4. What is the optimal soil pH range for musk cultivation?
   a) 5.5-6.5 b) 6.0-7.0
   c) 7.0-8.0 d) 8.0-9.0
5. How many irrigations are required for musk cultivation?
   a) 4-5 b) 6-7
   c) 8-9 d) 10-11
6. What is the recommended dose of NPK fertilizers for musk cultivation?
   a) 20, 20, 20 kg/ha b) 40, 30, 30 kg/ha
   c) 60, 40, 40 kg/ha d) 80, 50, 50 kg/ha
7. Which pest can damage musk plants by feeding on various parts during different stages of growth?
   a) Egyptian stem borer b) Pink bollworm
   c) Cotton semi-looper d) All of the above
8. How is musk seed oil obtained?
   a) Steam distillation of whole seeds
   b) Solvent extraction of ground seeds
   c) Cold pressing of whole seeds
   d) Enfleurage of whole seeds
9. What is the average seed yield of musk per hectare?
   a) 0.5 tonnes/ha b) 1 tonne/ha
   c) 1.5 tonnes/ha d) 2 tonnes/ha

10. How long can musk seeds be stored?

 a) 3 months b) 6 months

 c) 9 months d) 1 year

Short answer questions

1. Describe the different uses of musk plants, including medicinal, culinary, and fragrant properties.
2. Explain the ideal climate and soil requirements for musk cultivation.
3. Outline the process of musk seed oil production, including steam distillation and solvent extraction.
4. Describe the common pests and diseases that affect musk plants and their management practices.
5. Explain the importance of proper post-harvest handling and storage of musk seeds.

Answers for MCQ

1. *Abelmoschus moschatus*
2. Malvaceae
3. 20-45°C
4. 6.0-7.0
5. 6-7
6. 40, 30, 30 kg/ha
7. All of the above
8. Steam distillation of whole seeds
9. 1 tonne/ha
10. 6 months

References

Akbar, S. and Akbar, S., 2020. Abelmoschus moschatus Medik (Malvaceae) (Syn.: Hibiscus abelmoschus L.). Handbook of 200 Medicinal Plants: A Comprehensive Review of Their Traditional Medical Uses and Scientific Justifications, pp.15-19.

Akbar, S., 2020. Handbook of 200 medicinal plants: a comprehensive review of their traditional medical uses and scientific justifications.

Datta, A.K., Dubey, P.K., Mandal, A., Saha, A. and Sengupta, S., 2011. An Updated Overview on Abelmoschus moschatus. Journal of Tropical Medicinal Plants, 12(1).

Rajeswari, R. and Arumugam Shakila, A.S., 2015. Effect of integrated nutrient management practices on yield characters of ambrette (Abelmoschus moschatus Medic.).

Rajeswari, R. and Shakila, A., Influence of season and spacing on growth and yield performance of ambrette (Abelmoschus moschatus medic.). Recent Innovations in, p.183.

18

Patchouli

Scientific name: *Pogostemon cablin* Benth.

Family: Lamiaceae

Patchouli (*Pogostemon cablin*) is a perennial herb native to Southeast Asia, commonly found in India, China, and Indonesia. This fragrant herb has been used for centuries in traditional medicine, perfumery, and spiritual practices. Patchouli leaves are ovate-shaped, with a rough texture and a powerful, earthy fragrance. The leaves are steam-distilled to produce a rich, dark green essential oil with a distinctive scent. Patchouli is known for its anti-inflammatory, antiseptic, and antifungal properties, making it a popular ingredient in aromatherapy, skincare, and insect repellents. In India, patchouli is considered a sacred herb and is often used in traditional Indian medicine, Ayurveda, and Hindu rituals and ceremonies.

Origin and distribution

Patchouli, a native plant of the Philippines and Indonesia, has been extensively cultivated in various regions. In Indonesia, patchouli cultivation began in Aceh, Sumatra, and later expanded to Java. In India, it is primarily grown in the coastal areas of Tamil Nadu, Karnataka, Assam, and West Bengal.

Botany

Patchouli is a small, bushy herb belonging to the mint family (Lamiaceae). It has distinct oval-shaped leaves that are leathery with toothed edges, and are pale to purplish-green in color, emitting a characteristic fragrance. The plant produces small, purple or white flowers arranged in spikes at the end of stems, which are square-shaped, hairy, and branched. Patchouli has fibrous and shallow roots, and grows up to 1 meter in height as a perennial herb. Notably, patchouli does not produce viable seeds, and is typically propagated through stem cuttings.

Climate and soil requirements

Patchouli requires a medium-type soil with a loamy and fine texture. The soil should be well-drained, as waterlogged conditions can lead to nematode attacks and root rot diseases. This partial shade-loving plant can thrive in partially shaded areas, making it an ideal intercrop or main crop.

Patchouli prefers a warm and humid climate, with optimal growth occurring in regions with evenly distributed rainfall ranging from 150-300 cm annually. The crop can be successfully grown under irrigation in areas with low rainfall. Ideal temperature and humidity conditions for patchouli cultivation are 24-28°C and 75% relative humidity, respectively. The crop can grow up to an altitude of 800-1000 meters above sea level.

Chemical constituents

Patchouli oil is rich in sesquiterpene compounds, primarily patchouli alcohol (patchoulol), a tricyclic sesquiterpene commonly used in perfumes, soaps, and cosmetics. Other sesquiterpene hydrocarbons, such as patchoulena, guaiene, and seychellena, contribute to the oil's distinct scent. Patchoulol and α-patchoulol are essential components in determining the quality of patchouli oil.

In addition to these primary constituents, patchouli oil also contains several minor sesquiterpene compounds, including caryophyllene, pogostol, and norpatchoulenol. The biological activity of patchouli oil is closely related to its chemical components, particularly patchoulol. Non-volatile components of patchouli essential oil include flavonoids, glycosides, triterpenes, lignins, aldehydes, organic acids, and other phytochemical compounds.

Additional uses and benefits

Patchouli oil has been used for centuries in traditional medicine, aromatherapy, and perfumery. Its antiseptic, anti-inflammatory, and antifungal properties make it an effective treatment for various skin issues, such as acne, eczema, and dermatitis. Patchouli oil is also used as a natural insect repellent and is often incorporated into insecticides and mosquito coils.

Varieties

The Central Institute of Medicinal and Aromatic Plants (CIMAP), Lucknow, has developed and recommended several improved varieties of patchouli. These include:

1. **CIM-Samarth:** A fast-growing variety that can thrive in both shady and open field conditions. It is tolerant to several diseases.
2. **CIM-Utkrisht:** A newly developed variety with higher production potential than CIM-Samarth. It can be cultivated in both shady and open field conditions.

Field preparation

To ensure optimal growth, two deep ploughings are recommended to create a fine-textured soil. The field should be properly leveled to prevent waterlogging and ensure uniform water distribution during irrigation.

Planting materials and techniques

Patchouli is typically propagated using rooted cuttings grown in a nursery. Cuttings are made from healthy main stems, 10-12 cm in length, with 3-4 nodes. Leaves are removed, and the cuttings are planted in the nursery in April-May. Cuttings can be grown in soil or polybags, with a well-mixed soil and FYM ratio of 1:1.

Transplanting

Transplanting rooted cuttings is best done during the monsoon season to ensure maximum establishment and minimize irrigation costs. Transplanting should be done at a spacing of 50 cm × 50 cm.

Irrigation

The first irrigation should be done immediately after transplanting, followed by irrigation as needed. Waterlogging should be avoided. Irrigation is done for 3-4 days every 15-20 days after planting, with a frequency of 8-15 days thereafter. Under drip irrigation, irrigation is provided for 30 minutes daily, increasing to 60 minutes in two installments during hot and dry seasons.

Manures and fertilizers

During field preparation, 10-15 tons of FYM/ha or 7 tons of vermicompost/ha should be applied. Fertilizer application should be based on soil test results. Patchouli requires high doses of urea and potassium, with lesser phosphorus requirements. The recommended NPK ratio is 150:50:50 kg/ha.

Weed management

Regular weeding is essential for proper growth and maximum yield. Weeding should be done as needed, especially during the first 40 days after transplanting.

Shading

Patchouli is a shade-loving plant and can be grown as an under crop in arecanut and coconut orchards. Suitable shade trees like Gliricidia or Erythrina can be planted in advance to provide necessary shade.

Plant protection

Plant protection measures are essential for patchouli crops. The major pests affecting this crop are leaf caterpillars and whiteflies, which can be controlled using insecticides.

Additionally, nematode problems can arise after 2-3 years of cropping, which can be managed using nematicides.

Fungal diseases like leaf blight, root rot, and wilt can also affect patchouli crops. These can be controlled by applying fungicides, either as a spray or soil drench, at regular intervals.

Harvesting

The crop is ready for its first harvest 5-6 months after transplanting, when the leaves turn pale green. Subsequent harvests can be done every three months. Harvesting should be done with a sharp cutting tool, 20-25 cm from the apex. New shoots emerge from the nodes, so cutting should not be done too low.

Yield

The yield under drip irrigation is nearly twice that of conventional methods. Under conventional irrigation, the average yield of green leaves is 20 tons (three cuttings) per hectare, while under drip irrigation, it is 40 tons (three cuttings) per hectare. As an intercrop, 4 tons of dry biomass per hectare per year can be expected.

Post harvest handling

After harvesting, the biomass is dried under shade for 4-5 days. A drying shed with a thatched roof and mud floor is constructed with a drying area of 100 square meters. Essential oil is extracted by steam distillation, requiring the cell walls of the leaves to be ruptured.

Curing

After cutting, the stem and leaves are spread out for curing in thin layers on a hard, dry surface in sheds, allowing free circulation of air. The drying process typically takes three days. Proper drying is crucial for oil quality. During the process, the material should be frequently turned over to promote even drying and prevent fermentation.

Distillation

The oil is distilled from air-dried herbs using steam or hydro distillation. The recovery of oil from shade-dried herbs varies between 2.5-3.5%. The distillation duration is 8-11 hours for complete oil recovery.

Storage and packing of oil

Ensure that the essential oil is free from water before storage. Store the oil in glass bottles or drums made of steel or aluminum, depending on the quantity. Fill the containers to the brim, tightly cap, and store them in a cool, dry, and dark place.

MCQ questions

1. What is the scientific name of the patchouli plant?
   a) *Pogostemon cablin* Benth. b) *Pogostemon heyneanus*
   c) *Pogostemon stellatus* d) *Pogostemon plectranthoides*
2. Which family does the patchouli plant belong to?
   a) Lamiaceae b) Malvaceae
   c) Fabaceae d) Solanaceae
3. What is the ideal temperature range for patchouli cultivation?
   a) 20-24°C b) 24-28°C
   c) 28-32°C d) 32-36°C
4. What is the recommended spacing for transplanting patchouli cuttings?
   a) 25 cm × 25 cm b) 50 cm × 50 cm
   c) 75 cm × 75 cm d) 100 cm × 100 cm
5. How many irrigations are required for patchouli cultivation after transplanting?
   a) 5-7 b) 8-10
   c) 10-12 d) 12-15
6. What is the recommended NPK ratio for patchouli cultivation?
   a) 100:50:50 kg/ha b) 150:50:50 kg/ha
   c) 200:50:50 kg/ha d) 250:50:50 kg/ha
7. What is the major pest affecting patchouli crops?
   a) Leaf caterpillars b) Whiteflies
   c) Nematodes d) All of the above
8. How is patchouli essential oil extracted?
   a) Steam distillation b) Solvent extraction
   c) Cold pressing d) Enfleurage
9. What is the recovery rate of patchouli oil from shade-dried herbs?
   a) 1.5-2.5% b) 2.5-3.5%
   c) 3.5-4.5% d) 4.5-5.5%

10. How should patchouli essential oil be stored?
    a) In glass bottles or drums made of steel or aluminum
    b) In plastic containers or polythene bags
    c) In wooden barrels or cardboard boxes
    d) In open containers or exposed to sunlight

Short answer questions

1. Describe the different uses of patchouli plants, including medicinal, culinary, and fragrant properties.
2. Explain the ideal climate and soil requirements for patchouli cultivation.
3. Outline the process of patchouli essential oil production, including steam distillation and curing.
4. Describe the common pests and diseases that affect patchouli plants and their management practices.
5. Explain the importance of proper post-harvest handling and storage of patchouli essential oil.

Answers for MCQ

1. a) Pogostemon cablin Benth.
2. a) Lamiaceae
3. b) 24-28°C
4. a) 25 cm × 25 cm
5. a) 5-7
6. b) 150:50:50 kg/ha
7. d) All of the above
8. a) Steam distillation
9. b) 2.5-3.5%
10. a) In glass bottles or drums made of steel or aluminum

References

Kumar, A., Sharma, N., Chanotiya, C. S. and Lal, R. K. (2024) 'The pharmacological potential and the agricultural significance of the aromatic crop Patchouli (Pogostemon cablin Benth.): A review', Ecological Frontiers, vol. 44, no. 6, pp. 1109-1118.

Pandey, S. K., Bhandari, S., Sarma, N., Begum, T., Munda, S., Baruah, J. and Lal, M. (2021) 'Essential oil compositions, pharmacological importance and agro technological practices of Patchouli (Pogostemon cablin Benth.): A review', Journal of Essential Oil Bearing Plants, vol. 24, no. 6, pp. 1212-1226.

Pandey, S. K., Sarma, N., Begum, T. and Lal, M. (2020) 'Standardization of different drying methods of fresh patchouli (Pogostemon cablin) leaves for high essential oil yield and quality', Journal of Essential Oil Bearing Plants, vol. 23, no. 3, pp. 484-492.

Swamy, M. K. and Sinniah, U. R. (2016) 'Patchouli (Pogostemon cablin Benth.): Botany, agrotechnology and biotechnological aspects', Industrial Crops and Products, vol. 87, pp. 161-176.

Verma, R. K., Kumar, V., Verma, R. P., Singh, V. R. and Srivastava, R. K. (2024) 'Production, economics, properties and industrial uses of essential oil of patchouli (Pogostemon cablin): A review', Journal of Medicinal and Aromatic Plants, vol. 46, no. 1, pp. 1-9.

19

Pyrethrum

Scientific name: *Chrysanthemum cinerariaefolium L.*

Family: Asteraceae

Pyrethrum (*Chrysanthemum cinerariaefolium* L.) is a hearty perennial flower that thrives in interesting and challenging environments. It has been used for centuries as a natural insecticide. The pyrethrum daisy was first documented 2000 years ago, during the Chou Dynasty in China.

Origin and distribution

Pyrethrum originated in China over 2000 years ago and was later introduced to East Africa, where it is currently grown in Kenya, Uganda, Tanzania, and Rwanda. It is also grown in Tasmania, Australia, Ecuador, and Papua New Guinea.

Botany

Pyrethrum is a white flower-headed, tufted perennial herbaceous plant. It possesses deeply lobed leaves and has a numerous and fibrous shallow root system that extends up to 30 cm. The plant features numerous fairly rigid stems that grow up to 50-80 cm in height, accompanied by blue-green, deeply divided leaves. Notably, these leaves are covered on both sides by a dense, woolly material.

Climate and soil

Pyrethrum requires deep soils rich in phosphorus, calcium, and magnesium with a soil pH of 5.0-6.5. The ideal climate has a minimum of 750 mm of rainfall well spread over the season. It thrives at high altitudes, above 2130 meters (7,000 feet) above sea level. Pyrethrum cannot tolerate waterlogging.

Chemical composition

Pyrethrum contains naturally occurring pyrethrins, which are esters of chrysanthemic acid and pyrethric acid. The typical proportion of Pyrethrins I to II is 0.2:2.8. The pyrethrins content is affected by changes in temperatures.

Season

Pyrethrum is typically planted at the beginning of the monsoon rains

Land preparation

The land should be well-tilled to allow easy penetration by roots. All weeds should be removed, and the soil should be fertilized with triple superphosphate. Steep slopes must be terraced or be avoided altogether. Pyrethrum should occupy the land for three or at most four years.

Planting material and planting technique

Pyrethrum should be planted early in the main rains. Planting later leads to poor establishment and yields. The planting material can be either splits or seeds. For splits, cut the roots to 4 inches, remove the old roots, and leave 6 inches of green top. Planting holes should be 4-6 inches deep, with a teaspoonful of triple superphosphate added and mixed with the soil. Plant the splits with the roots straight down, fill with soil, and press firmly.

Seeds should be sown evenly on finely tilled soil, 10 seeds per inch, in rows 0.5 inches deep and 6 inches apart. After sowing, cover the rows with grass, water, and remove the grass after germination. Seedlings take 3-4 months to mature, so sow 3-4 months before the long rains.

Seedlings from seedbeds should be transplanted when the soil is well moistened. Planting holes for seedlings should be shallower than those for splits. All other planting operations are the same as for planting splits.

The recommended spacing is 30 cm intra-row and 60 cm inter-row, which gives a plant population of approximately 22,000 plants per acre. Alternatively, a spacing of 30 cm intra-row and 90 cm inter-row can be used, resulting in a plant population of approximately 14,000 plants per acre.

Irrigation

Pyrethrum does not require irrigation if rainfall is well-distributed. However, under irrigated conditions, weekly irrigation during the peak season gives better results. The crop should be irrigated frequently during the dry months. The crop should also be irrigated after the fertilizer application.

Weeding

Pyrethrum fields must be kept clean, particularly when plants are young. Weeds can drastically reduce flower yields. Weeding should be carried out frequently, every 4 weeks, using small forked jembes to avoid root damage. When weeding, the soil should be drawn around the base of the plants.

Manuring

Phosphate fertilizers are recommended for use in pyrethrum growing. Triple superphosphate should be applied @ 125-150 kg/ha. Farmyard manure may also be used at the rate of 4 tonnes per acre or 10 tonnes per hectare on poor soils. The FYM should be applied three months before planting of the crop.

Cutting back

Pyrethrum plants require annual cutting back, ideally towards the end of the dry season, following the flower flush. This process involves using a sickle to remove all stalks, while preserving the leaves. The cutting should be done at an angle to facilitate water runoff. The removed stalks should be burned, as leaving them can create problems during weeding and potentially harbor pests and diseases. It is essential to avoid delaying the cutting back process until the rains commence, as this can lead to reduced yields. Following cutting back, the fields should be weeded, and the plants earthed up immediately.

Frost, hail storm, and drought hazards

Pyrethrum plants are sensitive to weather fluctuations. Frost can damage crops grown in low-lying areas, but irrigation can mitigate this issue. Young plants in nursery beds can be protected from frost using shading materials like hessian cloth or polythene. Hailstorms can cause bruising on flower discs, leading to a loss of pyrethrins. Drought can result in plant death, reduced yields, and lower pyrethrins content in the flowers.

Plant protection

Pyrethrum plants are susceptible to various pests and diseases, including insects, fungi, nematodes, and mites. These reduce flower yields and quality in both nurseries and growers' fields.

Insects such as pyrethrum thrips, onion thrips, and green peach aphids can cause significant damage. Thrips feed on growing tips, flowers, and leaves, while aphids attack young shoots, leaves, and stems.

Nematodes, particularly the root knot nematode, can cause significant damage to pyrethrum roots, stems, leaves, and flowers. Bud disease, root rot, and wilt are common diseases affecting pyrethrum plants. Bud disease is caused by fungi, while root rot and wilt are caused by fungi and nematodes.

Control measures include using healthy plants for splitting, dipping splits in fungicides, crop rotation, and using resistant varieties. Regular monitoring and prompt action can help prevent the spread of pests and diseases.

Harvesting

Pyrethrum plants flower within one year of transplanting. The crop gives a poor yield in the first year, with optimum yields obtained during the 2nd and 3rd year. In India, three harvests of flowers are obtained as the flowering in these areas continues for 9 months.

Yield and pyrethrin content

The average annual yield in Kashmir is about 250 kg/ha, against 500 kg/ha in Nilgiris. The yield in the first year is about 450 kg/ha. The total pyrethrin content is reported to be 1.0-1.5% in India.

Postharvest handling

The harvested flower-heads are usually dried immediately in the sun. They are thinly spread on straw mats and turned over frequently to avoid fermentation. Dehydration is complete in 5-7 days. The ideal method of drying is to use hot-air driers, in which the temperature should not exceed 80°C.

MCQ questions

1. Where did pyrethrum originate over 2000 years ago?
   - a) East Africa
   - b) China
   - c) India
   - d) Australia
2. What is the ideal soil pH for growing pyrethrum?
   - a) 4.0-5.0
   - b) 5.0-6.5
   - c) 6.5-7.5
   - d) 7.5-8.5
3. How often should pyrethrum fields be weeded?
   - a) Every 2 weeks
   - b) Every 4 weeks
   - c) Every 6 weeks
   - d) Every 8 weeks
4. What is the recommended rate of triple superphosphate application?
   - a) 125-150kg/ha
   - b) 25-50 kg/ha
   - c) 500-750 kg/ha
   - d) No application needed
5. How many harvests of flowers are obtained in India?
   - a) 1
   - b) 2
   - c) 3
   - d) 4
6. What is the average annual yield of pyrethrum?
   - a) 250 kg/ha
   - b) 500 kg/ha
   - c) 700 kg/ha
   - d) 1000 kg/ha

7. What is the ideal method of drying harvested flower-heads?
   a) Sun drying b) Hot-air drying
   c) Shade drying d) Machine drying
8. What is the typical proportion of Pyrethrins I to II?
   a) 0.2:2.8 b) 0.5:1.5
   c) 1.0:2.0 d) 2.0:3.0
9. How often should pyrethrum plants be irrigated during the peak season?
   a) Daily b) Weekly
   c) Bi-weekly d) Monthly
10. What is the recommended spacing for pyrethrum plants?
    a) 20 cm intra-row and 40 cm inter-row
    b) 30 cm intra-row and 60 cm inter-row
    c) 40 cm intra-row and 80 cm inter-row
    d) 50 cm intra-row and 100 cm inter-row

Short answer questions

1. What are the ideal climate conditions for growing pyrethrum?
2. What are the common pests and diseases affecting pyrethrum plants?
3. What is the importance of cutting back pyrethrum plants?
4. How does temperature affect the pyrethrins content in pyrethrum flowers?
5. What is the recommended method for drying harvested pyrethrum flower-heads to preserve their quality?

Answeres for MCQ

1. b) China
2. b) 5.0-6.5
3 b) Every 4 weeks
4. a) 125-150 kg/ha
5. c) 3
6. a) 250 kg/ha
7. b) Hot-air drying
8. a) 0.2:2.8
9. b) Weekly
10. b) 30 cm intra-row and 60 cm inter-row

References

Ardelean, A.E. and Morar, G., 2010. Researches regarding plant growth biology of Chrysanthemum cinerariaefolium (Trev.) Vis. in its first year of vegetation.

Venkatabaman, T.M., 1949. Pyrethrum (Chrysanthemum Cinerariaefolium). Indian Journal of Horticulture, 6(3and4), pp.22-27.

Verma, P.P.S., Kumar, D., Agri, B., Padalia, R.C. and Kumar, A., 2023. Flower Yield Potential of Pyrethrum (Chrysanthemum cinerariaefolium L.) under Various NPK Levels in the Lower Hills of Uttarakhand, India. Journal of Agricultural Sciences (Sri Lanka), 18(3).

Verma, P.P.S., Padalia, R.C. and Singh, V.R., 2017. Effect of Nitrogen, Phosphorus and Potassium Levels on Growth and Flower Yield of Pyrethrum (Chrysanthemum Cinerariaefolium) Under Western Himalayan Region of Uttrakhand. International Journal of Agriculture Innovations and Research, 6, pp.2319-73.

Wandahwa, P., Van Ranst, E. and Van Damme, P., 1996. Pyrethrum (Chrysanthemum cinerariaefolium Vis.) cultivation in West Kenya: origin, ecological conditions and management. Industrial Crops and Products, 5(4), pp.307-322.

20

Vetiver

Scientific name: *Vetiveria zizanioides* L.

Family: Poaceae

Vetiver, scientifically known as *Vetiveria zizanioides* L., is a tropical grass species belonging to the Poaceae family. Native to India and Southeast Asia, Vetiver is a perennial grass that grows up to 2 meters in height, with long, thin leaves and a deep, fibrous root system. Vetiver is highly valued for its essential oil, which is extracted from its roots and used in perfumery, aromatherapy, and traditional medicine. The plant is also known for its soil-stabilizing properties, making it an effective tool for erosion control and land conservation.

Origin and distribution

Vetiver is native to the tropical regions of Asia, specifically India, Pakistan, Bangladesh, Sri Lanka, and Malaysia. It is cultivated and produced in many parts of the world, including Tropical Asia, Africa, Australia, Haiti, Indonesia, Guatemala, India, China, and Brazil. Vetiver is also grown in several other countries, such as the Philippines, Japan, Angola, Dominican Republic, Argentina, and Jamaica. The global production of Vetiver is estimated to be around 250 tons per annum. In India, Vetiver grows wild in various states, including Punjab, Uttar Pradesh, and Assam.

Botany

Vetiver is a perennial, tufted bunchgrass that grows up to 1.5 meters (5 feet) in height. The plant has a robust, erect habit with a dense cluster of stems arising from a short, woody rhizome. The leaves are thin, linear, and rigid, with a length of up to 100 cm (3.3 feet) and a width of about 0.5-1.5 cm (0.2-0.6 inches). They are erect, with a sharp tip and a smooth, glabrous surface. The stems are also erect and rigid, with a diameter of up to 1 cm (0.4 inches), and bear small, brown-purple flowers in long spikes. The inflorescence is a long, narrow spike that can grow up to 30 cm (12 inches) in length, bearing numerous small, brown-purple flowers arranged in a dense, alternate pattern. The roots are long, thin, and fragrant, growing downward in the soil to depths of more than 3 meters (10 feet), with numerous rootlets that absorb water and nutrients from the soil. Vetiver is highly drought-resistant, thanks to its deep, extensive root system, and can survive for long periods without water.

Climate and soil

Vetiver is a highly adaptable plant that can thrive in a wide range of temperatures, from -1°C to 56°C. The ideal soil temperature for Vetiver growth is 25°C. However, the plant roots may become dormant if the temperature drops below 5°C. Vetiver is also sensitive to frost, which can cause the shoots to become dormant and eventually die. Nevertheless, the underground growing points can survive and regrow quickly when the climate improves. Vetiver prefers partial shading, but it can tolerate full sun with proper care. The plant is highly resilient and can survive drought, floods, and moderate humidity, making it an ideal crop for areas with average rainfall of at least 1500 mm.

Vetiver can grow in various soils but prefers well-drained, sandy loam or red soil rich in organic matter. Clay loam soil is also suitable, but clayey soil should be avoided. Vetiver can tolerate saline or alkaline soils with a pH range of 8-10. However, it's essential to ensure proper drainage and avoid waterlogging, especially during the initial stages of growth. Mature Vetiver plants can survive waterlogging and even absorb heavy metals from dissolved water.

Chemical constituents

Vetiver contains diverse chemical constituents that contribute to its unique properties and uses. The major active constituents identified in Vetiver include khusimol, vetivone, eudesmol, khusimone, zizaene, and prezizaene, which are considered the "fingerprint" of Vetiver oil. This oil is highly valued in perfumery and aromatherapy and is composed of a complex mixture of over 150 sesquiterpenoid constituents. Alpha-vetivone, beta-vetivone, and khusimol are the most prominent compounds, occurring in amounts up to 35%. The composition and odor quality of Vetiver oil vary depending on its origin. Other notable chemical constituents present in Vetiver include vetiverol, terpenes, benzoic acid, and several others.

Varieties

CIMAP-31: Released by the Central Institute of Medicinal and Aromatic Plants (CIMAP) in 1994, this variety is known for its high oil yield and improved quality.

CIMAP-36: Another variety released by CIMAP in 1997, CIMAP-36 is characterized by its high oil content and resistance to diseases.

CIMAP-39: Released in 2001, CIMAP-39 is a high-yielding variety with improved oil quality and resistance to pests and diseases.

Pant Vetiver-1: Developed by the G.B. Pant University of Agriculture and Technology, this variety is known for its high oil yield and improved quality.

VL-9: Released by the Indian Institute of Horticultural Research, VL-9 is a high-yielding variety with improved oil quality and resistance to diseases.

Vetiver-38: Developed by the Tamil Nadu Agricultural University, this variety is characterized by its high oil content and resistance to pests and diseases.

ODV-3 released from Kerala Agricultural University

Land preparation

The field should be cleared of perennial weeds and shrubs. The land is deep tilled, and final land preparation is done with the onset of pre-monsoon showers. Fields are laid out into beds of convenient size for uniform cropping and higher root yield.

Season

The ideal time for commercial cultivation of Vetiver is with the pre-monsoon shower, from April to August. In South India, the best planting time for higher oil yield is June-July. In flood-affected areas, the crop should be established before the floodwater submerges it, ideally 2 months before the normal flood.

Planting material and planting technique

Vetiver can be propagated through tillers and slips, with slips being the superior planting material. Slips are prepared by digging up and chopping the plants 25-30 cm above the ground. The clumps are divided into slips with 2-3 tillers, and the top of the slips are cut down before planting to prune transpiration loss. Slips are planted in pits 5-8 cm deep, with 2-3 slips per pit, and spaced 45 x 30 cm apart.

Irrigation

If planting is done during the rain-free period, the field should be irrigated immediately after planting. Although growth may be slow initially, the plants develop quickly once roots are established.

Weeding and intercultural operations

Initial growth of Vetiver is slow, allowing weeds to infest the inter-row space. 2-3 weedings are needed at an interval of about a month during the initial period of growth. Earthing up after weeding is beneficial to the crop, encouraging root growth at the crown. Shoot cutting is done twice during the crop cycle to increase tillering and root growth.

Manuring

Application of FYM @ 10 ton/ha and 60 kg of N, 22.5 kg each of P_2O_5 and K_2O/ha is recommended for increasing the yield of Vetiver. In poor soils, 40 kg each of nitrogen, phosphorus, and potassium per acre is applied before final ploughing. Top-dressing with 20 kg N/ha may be done 4 months after planting, depending on soil fertility and crop growth.

Plant protection

Vetiveria zizanioides is susceptible to pests like shoot borers, scale insects, aphids, and whiteflies, which can be controlled by spraying insecticides. Diseases like leaf spot, root rot, leaf blight, and rust can be managed by removing infected plants, improving air circulation, and applying fungicides. Regular monitoring and adopting integrated pest management practices can help prevent infestations and reduce damage to the crop.

Harvesting and cleaning process

Harvesting Vetiver roots is a crucial process that affects the yield and quality of the essential oil. The ideal time for harvesting is between 18 to 24 months after planting, with the best time being between December and February. If harvested early, the yield of essential oil is higher, but the oil lacks high boiling constituents. On the other hand, delaying the harvest until 24 months improves the quality of the oil but decreases the yield.

The harvesting process involves cutting the stem portion at a 15-20 cm height and uprooting the clumps along with the roots. This is typically done manually, but mechanical harvesting using a tractor-drawn single disc can increase root recovery by 16%. The clumps are then beaten on a log to remove adhering earth, and the roots are separated from the plants using a sharp knife.

After harvesting, the roots are washed gently in clean running water to remove adhering earth. The cleaned roots are then dried on drying grounds and turned over regularly until dry. Foreign matter is removed during this process. The cleaned and dried roots are then sent to the distillery or storage shed, where they are allowed to mature. Drying under shade for 1-2 days improves the olfactory quality of the essential oil, while prolonged sun drying reduces oil yield. Dry roots can be stored in shade for 60-70 days without loss of oil, and the quality improves appreciably.

Yield

Several factors, including age, soil, climatic conditions, and strain, influence Vetiver roots' yield. On average, one hectare of Vetiver plantation yields 5-7 tons of roots. Upon distillation, these roots yield 15-16 kg of oil. The oil content of Vetiver roots ranges from 1.00 to 1.50% on a dry-weight basis. The resulting oil is light yellow in color and contains 65-75% vetiverol.

Oil extraction

The essential oil of Vetiver is extracted from its roots through steam distillation. Freshly harvested roots yield more oil than stored roots, with the yield decreasing progressively with storage time. The roots are soaked in water for 18-20 hours before distillation to facilitate oil release. Cutting the roots into 2.5-5 cm lengths can also increase oil recovery.

The distillation process typically lasts for 20-24 hours, as the valuable quality constituents are contained in the high-boiling fractions. Two fractions of oil are obtained during distillation: lighter and heavier oils. To prevent loss of the lighter fraction, a piece of marking cloth is tied at the delivery outlet, which traps the oil and allows it to be collected. Traditionally, copper vessels with stainless steel condensers are used for Vetiver distillation, as the oil reacts with free copper to produce a bluish color that is highly valued in perfumery.

The distillation technique significantly influences the quality of Vetiver oil. Adjusting steam pressure and post-harvest treatment of roots can improve both yield and quality. The oil quality is also governed by varietal selection, harvesting at the proper age (15-18 months), and during the dry period only. Ideally, the oil should contain a minimum of 14% Khusimol and low levels of caryophyllene.

After oil extraction, the leftover roots can be used to create various bi-products, such as cartons, mats, and handicraft items. A tasty and refreshing syrup can also be prepared using the water obtained during distillation.

MCQ questions

1. What is the main constituent responsible for the unique fragrance of Vetiver oil?

   a) Vetiverol   b) Khusimol

   c) Caryophyllene   d) Patchoulol

2. Which family does the Vetiver plant belong to?

   a) Poaceae   b) Lamiaceae

   c) Malvaceae   d) Fabaceae

3. What is the ideal temperature range for Vetiver cultivation?

   a) 20-30°C   b) 25-35°C

   c) 15-25°C   d) 5-15°C

4. How often should Vetiver be irrigated?
   a) Every 7-10 days b) Every 10-15 days
   c) Every 15-20 days d) Every 20-25 days
5. What is the recommended NPK ratio for Vetiver cultivation?
   a) 60:22.5:22.5 kg/ha b) 80:25:25 kg/ha
   c) 100:30:30 kg/ha d) 120:35:35 kg/ha
6. How many weedings are needed during the initial period of Vetiver growth?
   a) 1-2 b) 2-3
   c) 3-4 d) 4-5
7. What is the ideal time for harvesting Vetiver roots?
   a) 12-18 months after planting b) 18-24 months after planting
   c) 24-30 months after planting d) 30-36 months after planting
8. How is Vetiver essential oil extracted?
   a) Steam distillation b) Solvent extraction
   c) Cold pressing d) Enfleurage
9. What is the average yield of Vetiver roots per hectare?
   a) 3-5 tons b) 5-7 tons
   c) 7-9 tons d) 9-11 tons
10. What is the recommended storage duration for dried Vetiver roots?
   a) 30-60 days b) 60-90 days
   c) 90-120 days d) 120-150 days

Short answer questions

1. Describe the different uses of Vetiver plants, including medicinal, culinary, and fragrant properties.
2. Explain the ideal climate and soil requirements for Vetiver cultivation.
3. Outline the process of Vetiver essential oil production, including steam distillation and root harvesting.
4. Describe the common pests and diseases that affect Vetiver plants and their management practices.
5. Explain the importance of proper post-harvest handling and storage of Vetiver roots.

Answers for MCQ

1. b) Khusimol
2. a) Poaceae
3. b) 25-35°C
4. b) Every 10-15 days
5. a) 60:22.5:22.5 kg/ha
6. b) 2-3
7. b) 18-24 months after planting
8. a) Steam distillation
9. b) 5-7 tons
10. a) 30-60 days

References

Ingole, S.N., 2019. An Overview of Vetiveria zizanioides (Linn.) Nash (Poaceae). Ethnobotany: Local Knowledge and Traditions, p.1962.

Maffei, M., 2002. The Genus Vetiveria. London: Taylor and Francis.

Mishra Snigdha, M.S., Kumar, S.S., Mohapatra Sharmistha, M.S. and Chauhan Deepa, C.D., 2013. An overview on Vetiveria zizanioides.

Momin, K.C., Devi, N.S., Dobhal, S., John, A., Shadap, A. And Lego, N., The agrotechnology of some aromatic crops. Aromatic plants, p.83.

Rao, R.R. and Suseela, M.R., 2000. Vetiveria zizanioides (Linn.) Nash–a multipurpose eco-friendly grass of India. ICV-2 held in Cha-am, Phetchaburi, Thailand, pp.18-22.

21

Salaparni

Scientific name: *Pseudarthria viscida* L.

Family: Fabaceae

Pseudarthira viscida is an important plant in the Indian conventional system of medicine. It is known as salaparni in Sanskrit, belongs to the Fabaceae family, and is distributed in peninsular India and Srilanka. It is among the dasamoola, a combination of roots of ten medicinal plants. It is used as a medicine for the treatment of various diseases due to its versatile nature and it is also an essential ingredient of various ayurvedic formulations such as Surasadi Thailam,Sudarsanasava, Balajeerakadhi Kashayam,Brihatyadi Kashayam, Surasadi Kashayam,Brahmarasayana. *Pseudarthria viscida* is a herbal plant that exhibits pharmacological andtherapeutic properties. It is widely used in ayurveda alone or poly-herbal formulations to treat various diseases. The whole plant is known for antipyretic, analgesic, antioxidant and anti-fungal effects. It is commercially and extensively used to treat tuberculosis, hemorrhoids, blood disorders, tumors, diabetes, hyperthermia and bronchitis. The root is the economic part, which alleviates tridoshas, namely vata, pitta, andcoupha. The roots are with thermogenic, astringent, emollient, digestive, febrifuge andcardiotonic. Majorchemical compounds present in the roots aregallic acid, caffeic acid, rutin, quercetin, ferulicacid and phenolic compounds and also reported with proteins, flavonoids and leucopelargonidin. Roots are well known for anthelmintic,anti-diuretic and anti-inflammatory properties. Decoction of the root used against heart diseases, rheumatism, asthma and piles. *Pseudarthria viscida* is becoming extinct from nature, and its number has been reduced drastically. Due to the limited availability *of Pseudarthria viscida,* which is substituted by other leguminous trifoliate plant species such as *Desmodiumpulchellum* and Uraria rufescens. There for, it is put in the red list category and the plant requires proper management practices to exploit its therapeutic potential in the treatment of various diseases.

Chemical constituents

Photochemical screening indicates the presence of flavonoids, alkaloids, saponins,tannins and phenolic compounds in *Pseudarthria viscida.*

Structurally, they are phenol groups that serve asa source of readily available hydrogen atoms such that the subsequent radicals produced can be delocalized over the phenol structure. Extracts of *Pseudarthria viscida* possess surfactant properties due to the presence of saponin, such as diosgenin. Flavonoids and phenolic compounds present inthe extract of *Pseudarthria viscida* helps in the bio-reduction of Ag + to Ag 0). Chemical constituentssuch as vaccenic acid, gamma sitosterol andstigma sterol were identified from the roots ofPseudarthria viscida. Roots of Pseudarthriaviscida contain phytochemical constituents suchas caffeic acid, gallic acid, rutin and ferulic acid. Compounds such as 1, 5 dicaffeoylquinicacid, oleic acid, tetradecanoic acid and quercetin are primarily present in the roots of *Pseudarthria viscida*. Qualitative analysis reveals the presence of triterpenoids, proteins and amino acids. The extract of *Pseudarthria viscida* is used to synthesize silver nano particles due to the presence of citric and ascorbic acids.

Origin and distribution

Pseudarthria viscida is native to Malaysia, India and Myanmar. It is also found in Sri Lanka. In India it is found in the states of Odessa, Tamil Nadu, Kerala, Andhra Pradesh and Gujarat. In Karnataka, it is found in the districts of Bidar, Ballari,Belagavi, and Bengaluru. In Telengana, it is found in the districts of Nalgonda, Khammam and Mehboobnagar.

Botany

Pseudarthria viscida is a perennial diffuse sub-shrub plant that can attain a height of one meter. Branches are slender, covered with greyish-white hairs. Leaves are trifoliate,compound and hairy. Leaflets are broadly ovate and densely hairy. Petioles are half to one inch long. Flowers are small, purpleand found on terminal or axillary racemes. Seeds are brownish black in colour. Each pod contains 4 to 6 seeds. Seeds have a reniform structure.

Climate and soil

Pseudarthria viscida can thrives in tropical and subtropical regions. It requires an optimum temperature of 20-35^0 C. The plant prefers moderate to high rainfall. *Pseudarthria viscida* grows well in areas with well distributed rainfall but can tolerate occasional dry spells. The plant requires full to partial sunlight. Pseudarthria viscida can tolerate partial shade, but it prefers open areas for better growth. Well-drained, loamy to sandy loam soil is ideal for the growth of plant. *Pseudarthria viscida* grows well in soil with moderate fertility and a pH of 6.0 -7.5. The plant requires moist soil but it cannot withstand water logging.

Season

Start of the rainy season in May-June.

Land preparation

Before sowing, you can plow and level the field. Before sowing the field should be ploughed and leveled. Then, broadcast the seeds at the beginning of the monsoon. The crop should be maintained without weed competition.

Planting material and Planting techniques

Pseudarthria viscida is commonly propagated by seeds. There are some limited factors for commercial cultivation such as low seed viability, low germination rate, and high mortality of the seedling at the young stage. The sprouting percentage is influenced by genetic and environmental factors. In such a condition clonal propagation allows rapid production of large quantities of high-quality planting material. Usually branch, stem and nodal cuttings are used for clonal multiplication.

The cotyledonary node and young leaf pieces are used as explants for callus induction and shoot regeneration and adventitious root induction from the shoot. MS medium gave a successful result in in-vitro culture. NAA (Naphthalene Acetic Acid and BAP (6-Benzyl Amino Purine) combination are best for callus induction and indirect organogenesis. BAP is good for shoot induction. Developed plantlets are transferred to greenhouse and then to natural conditions.

Irrigation

Irrigation is not essential during the monsoon, but you can provide it during droughts conditions like once in a week.

Weeding

Intercropping can reduce weed growth by using beneficial plants to fill vacant spaces. Maintain the crop without weeds. Weeding should be done between 20-24 weeks after planting.

Manures and fertilizers

Manure/fertilizer application is done ideally after soil/plant analysis. Since the plant can fix nitrogen, organic matter is enough for this crop. A balanced application of fertilizers such as compost or farmyard manure helps in promoting growth.

Harvesting

After one year of planting, you can harvest the roots that are 15 cm long. The roots will be ready for harvesting after one year of planting. The plants are uprooted manually. The roots attaining 15 cm length are harvested after one year. Mature plants bearing the seeds are retained to get natural regeneration. Hence it reduces the cost of planting.

Post harvest handling

Collected roots are cleaned and dried in shade. Large stems and roots are cut into smaller pieces for uniform drying and further processing. Dried plant material can be powdered depending on the use.

Yield

Yield may vary from 750 to 850 kilos of dried roots per hectare. Soil, fertility, climate conditions, pest and disease management and harvesting time are the factors that affect the yield. Intercropping and crop rotation can increase the yield.

MCQ questions

1. What is the scientific name of the Moovila plant?
   a) *Atropa belladonna* L.
   b) *Centella asiatica* (L) Urban
   c) *Piper nigrum* L.
   d) *Pseudarthira viscida* L.
2. Which family *Pseudarthira viscida* belongs to?
   a) Fabaceae
   b) Solanaceae
   c) Asteraceae
   d) Apiaceae
3. What is the ideal time of planting *Pseudarthira viscida*?
   a) Late spring
   b) Start of rainy season
   c) Before spring
   d) After summer
4. How long it take for *Pseudarthira viscida* to mature?
   a) 6-8 months
   b) 8-10 months
   c) 1 year
   d) 12-14 months
5. When is the period of weeding in *Pseudarthira viscida*?
   a) 1st-4th week after planting
   b) 15-20 days after planting
   c) 20th-24th week after planting
   d) 28th-32nd week after planting

6. What is the recommended dose of manure for *Pseudarthira viscida*?
   a) 5-10 tonnes/ha b) 10-15 tonnes/ha
   c) No manure is needed d) 20-25 tonnes/ha
7. How often should *Pseudarthira viscida* be watered?
   a) Regular watering b) Every other day
   c) Once a week d) Once a month
8. What is the method of harvesting used in *Pseudarthira viscida*?
   a) Mechanical harvesting b) Combine harvesting
   c) Manual harvesting
9. Which part of *Pseudarthira viscida* plant is used for propagation?
   a) Seeds b) Stems
   c) Leaves d) Fruits
10. What is the approximate yield potential of *Pseudarthira viscida*?
   a) 10-12 tonnes/ha b) 750-850kg/ha
   c) 20-25 tonnes/ha d) 25-30 tonnes/ha

Short answer questions

7. Explain soil and climate conditions for Pseudarthira viscida
8. Give an account on the cultivation practices for Pseudarthira viscida
9. Explain method of harvesting
10. Describe the chemical constituents in Pseudarthira viscida
11. Explain the method of manuring and land preparation in Pseudarthira viscida crops

Answers for MCQ

1 d) *Pseudarthira viscida L.*
2. a) Fabaceae
3. b) Start of rainy season
4. c) 1 year
5. c) 20th-24th weeks after planting
6. c) no manure is required
7. c) once a week
8. c) manual harvesting
9. a) seeds
10. b) 750-850kg/ha

References

Hanish Singh, J.C., Alagarsamy, V., Parthiban, P., Selvakumar, P. and Narsimha Reddy, Y (2011) Neuroprotective potential of ethanolic extract of Pseudarthriaviscida (L.) Wight &Arn. Against β-amyloid(25-35)-induced amnesiain mice. Indian Journal of Biochemistry and Biophysics48: 197-201.

Muthukrishnan, S. and Thinakaran, R. (2012) Chemicalinvestigation of Pseudarthriaviscida root byGC-MSanalysis. PharmacognosyCommunications2(3): 26-29.

Vijayabaskaran, M., Sajeer, P. and Perumal, P. (2011) Wound healing activity of ethanol extract of Pseudarthriaviscida Linn. International Research Journal of Pharmacy 2(4): 141-44.

Dimo, T., Fotio, A.L., Nguelefack, T.B., Asongalem, E.A. and Kamtchouing, P. (2006) Anti-inflammatory activity of leaf extracts of Kalanchoe crenata Andr. Indian Journal of Pharmacology 38: 115.

Winter, C.A., Risley, E.A. and Nuss, G.W. (1980) Carrageenin-induced edema in hind paw of the rat as an assay for anti-inflammatory drugs. Proceedings of the Society for Experimental BiologyandMedicine111(3): 544-547.

Nithyakalyani, K. (2020) Phytochemical and pharmacological investigations of Pseudarthriaviscida (L.) Wight andArnott. Int. J. Pharmacometrics and Integrated Biosci5(2): 16-21.

22

Centella

Scientific name: *Centella asiatica* (L) Urban

Fmily: Apiaceae

The plant *Centella asiatica* belongs to the family Apiaceae. *C. asiatica* widely distributed throughout tropical and subtropical regions of the world. Commonly known as Gotu Kola, Indian pennywort or Asiatic pennywort. It has a long history of utilization in Chinese and Ayurvedic traditional medicines since centuries. Leaves are yellowish-green color, thin and edible. The plant grows horizontally through its stolones which roots in underground. *C. asiatica* shows a wide range of biological activities such as anti-inflammatory, anti-ulcer, wound healing, anti-psoriatic, anti-convulsant, hepato protective, immuno-stimulant, anti-diabetic, sedative, anti-bacterial, anti-viral, anti-tumor, cardio protective and anti-oxidant activities.

Origin and distribution

C. asiatica widely distributed throughout tropical and subtropical regions of the world. *C. asiatica* is widely found in Sree Lanka, India, Indonesi, Malaeysia and China. It is especially common in the Indian sub continent. It is also present in Eastern and Northern parts of Australia. It may also found in Tropical parts of Africa and Madagascar. *C. asiatica* has been introduced and is now cultivated or found in Thailand, Cambodia, Vietnam, The Philippines, Myanmar, and Brazil. Beyond Madagascar it is found in parts of Southern and Central Africa. The plant grows in countries such as Hawaii and Fiji. It is also found in Southern states like Florida.

Botany

The plant prefers habitats such as wetlands, riverbanks, and marshy areas. The plant grows typically 2-6inches tall. Roots are fibrous spread laterally across the ground. The stems are thin, elongated and creepy, produces stolons that are grows along the ground. It usually produces nodes and internodes. At each nodes, adventitious roots are form. Leaves are arranged solitary or in a cluster of 1-5 at each node. Leaves are soft, smooth, papery and bright green to dark green in colour. Leaf margin is slightly crenate and sometimes cleft at the base of the leaf base. The lamina is wide, round to kidney-shaped and have a rounded serrated tip. The tiny flower grows in a small cluster of 3 to 5 flowers. Each flower is enclosed in two green bracts. Flowers are typically pinkish, light purple or greenish white in colour. Corolla with 5 tiny petals, oval to triangular in shape. Calyx contains 5 very small sepals. Flowers are hermaphroditic, it contains both stamens and pistils as their reproductive organs. The fruit is a Schizocarp.

Climate and soil

The plant usually grows in moist, fertile, and sandy loam. Clayey soil with good moisture and organic matter suits well for the crop. *Centella asiatica* thrives best in monsoon periods or in well drained beds. The plant prefers acidic soils than the alkaline soils.

Chemical constituents

The plant *C. asiatica* contains many compounds belonging to different chemical classes. The medicinal properties of the plant are due to its biologically active components of tri-terpenes, and saponins. The tri-terpenes are composed of compounds like Asiaticosside, Asiatic acid, Madecassoside, Madecassic acid, Brahmoside, Brahminoside, Brahmic acid, Centelloside, Centic acid, Madasiatic acid, Thankiniside, Isothankunisode and Cenellic acid. The content of tri-terpene components can be affected by the location and divers environmental conditions.

Season

The best season to plant *C. asiatica* is in late spring or early summer. Also sow seeds in the house during spring season.

Land preparation and Planting

The field is prepared by giving one ploughing and two harrowing followed by planting. The land is provided a thorough procedure by tillage of 4-6 ploughing and brought to fine tilth. After leveling, beds are prepared. The plant is propagated by rooted suckers and seeds. Nursery raised seedlings are also used for propagation.

Irrigation

Centella asiatica requires regular watering. During dry season fortnightly irrigation is needed and also need drainage during rainy seasons.

Manures and fertilizer

The manure FYM at the rate of 15-20tones/ha is mixed with soil at the time of field preparation. NPK fertilizer at 100:50:50 kg/ha in a four split doses are given. A balanced fertilizer is needed every 4-6 weeks during the growing season.

Weeding

Regular weeding is needed at the initial months. Initially hand weeding is provided for *Centella asiatica* crops at an interval of 15-20 days. Later after the proliferation of plant forms dense vegetation, weeding is provided according to its requirement.

Plant protection

No disease and pests are seen in the crop. To protect the plant Centella asiatica, a regular weeding is needed. Use plant growth promoting rhizobacteria (PGPR) and shoot tip culture practices improves the crop production.

Harvesting

The crop of *Centella asiatica* matures in 90 days after planting. It is harvested through hand-cutting method (Manual harvesting) at fully grown leaf stage. Intermittent harvesting is provided at fortnightly intervals to get the outer leaves from January onwards from growing branches. The harvesting of bulk material should be done on the month of June, before monsoon. A few stolons are left as such in the field for regeneration of which the further harvest starts from October onwards. The leaves are harvested sunny weather to facilitate drying.

Yield

As a pure crop 10-12 tones/ha yield is obtained on three harvests in an year. The yield become decline after second year and needed fresh planting.

From the harvested plant unwanted materials are sorted out and dried in shade.

MCQ questions

1. What is the scientific name of the Kudangal plant?

   a) *Atropa belladonna* L. b) *Centella asiatica* (L) Urban

   c) *Piper nigrum* L. d) *Capsicum annuum* L

2. Which family *Centella asiatica* belongs to?

   a) Fabaceae b) Solanaceae

   c) Asteraceae d) Apiaceae

3. What is the ideal time of planting *Centella asiatica*?

   a) Late spring or early summer b) During summer

   c) Before spring d) After summer

4. How long it take for *asiatica* to mature?
   a) 6-8 months b) 8-10 months
   c) 90 days d) 12-14 months

5. When is the period of weeding in *Centella asiatica*?
   a) 1st-4th week after planting
   b) 15-20 days after planting
   c) 20th-24th week after planting
   d) 28th-32nd week after planting

6. What is the recommended dose of manure for *Centella asiatica*?
   a) 5-10 tonnes/ha b) 10-15 tonnes/ha
   c) 15-20 tonnes/ha d) 20-25 tonnes/ha

7. How often should *Centella asiatica* be watered?
   a) Regular watering b) Every other day
   c) Once a week d) Once a month

8. What is the method of harvesting used in *Centella asiatica*?
   a) Mechanical harvesting b) Combine harvesting
   c) Manual harvesting

9. Which part of *Centella asiatica* plant is used for propagation?
   a) Roots or seeds b) Stems
   c) Leaves d) Fruits

10. What is the approximate yield potential of *Centella asiatica*?
   a) 10-12 tonnes/ha b) 15-20 tonnes/ha
   c) 20-25 tonnes/ha d) 25-30 tonnes/ha

Short answer questions

11. Explain soil and climate conditions for *Centella asiatica*
12. Give an account on the cultivation practices for *Centella asiatica*
13. Explain method of harvesting
14. Describe the chemical constituents in *Centella asiatica*
15. Explain the method of manuring and land preparation in *Centella asiatica* crops

Answers for MCQ

1. b) Centella asiatica (L) Urban.
2. d) Apiaceae
3. a) Late spring or early summer
4. c) 90 days
5. b) 15-20 days after planting
6. c) 15-20tonnes/ha
7. a) Regular watering
8. c) Manual harvesting
9. a) Root and seeds
10. a) 10-12tonnes/ha

References

Bylka, W., Znajdek-Awiżeń, P., Studzińska-Sroka, E., Dańczak-Pazdrowska, A., & Brzezińska, M. (2014). Centella asiatica in dermatology: an overview. Phytotherapy research, 28(8), 1117-1124.

Chopra, R. N., Nayar, S. L., & Chopra, I. C. (1986). Glossary of Indian medicinal plants (including the supplement). Council of scientific and industrial research, New Delhi, 89, 77-100.

Howes M. J. R. and Houghton P., Plants used in Chinese and Indian traditional medicine for improvement of memory and cognitive function, Pharmacology Biochemistry and Behavior. (2003) 75, no. 3, 513–527

Murray, M. T., and Pizzorno, J. E. Jr (2012). Textbook of natural medicine. 4th ed. Eds. J. E. Pizzorno Jr. and T. Michael (Edinburgh: Churchill Livingstone), 650.

Tan, S.C.; Bhattamisra, S.K.; Chellappan, D.K.; Candasamy, M. Actions and Therapeutic Potential of Madecassoside and Other Major Constituents of Centella Asiatica: A Review. Appl. Sci. 2021, 11, 8475

23

Good Collection and Agricultural Practices (GCAP) in Medicinal and Aromatic Plants

Medicinal and Aromatic Plants (MAPs) are vital components of traditional medicine, perfumery, and cosmetics. To ensure the quality and sustainability of these plants, it is essential to adopt Good Collection and Agricultural Practices (GCAP). GCAP encompasses a set of guidelines and practices that promote the responsible cultivation, collection, and harvesting of MAPs.

Principles of GCAP

Sustainability: Ensure that the cultivation and collection of MAPs are sustainable and do not harm the environment or deplete natural resources.

Quality: Maintain the highest quality standards for MAPs, from cultivation to harvesting and processing.

Traceability: Ensure that MAPs are traceable from the farm to the consumer, to guarantee authenticity and quality.

Fair Trade: Promote fair trade practices, ensuring that farmers and collectors receive fair prices for their products.

Environmental Stewardship: Protect biodiversity, conserve water, and minimize waste and pollution.

Agricultural Practices

Soil Conservation: Implement soil conservation techniques, such as contour farming and mulching, to prevent soil erosion.

Irrigation Management: Use efficient irrigation systems and practices to conserve water and prevent overwatering.

Crop Rotation: Rotate crops to maintain soil fertility, reduce pests and diseases, and promote biodiversity.

Integrated Pest Management (IPM): Use IPM techniques, such as biological control and cultural controls, to minimize the use of chemical pesticides.

Organic Farming: Promote organic farming practices, such as the use of compost and manure, to reduce chemical inputs.

Collection and Harvesting Practices

Selective Harvesting: Harvest MAPs selectively, to avoid damaging the plant or the environment.

Timing of Harvest: Harvest MAPs at the optimal time, to ensure maximum quality and potency.

Drying and Processing: Dry and process MAPs immediately after harvesting, to prevent spoilage and contamination.

Cleaning and Grading: Clean and grade MAPs to remove impurities and ensure uniform quality.

Post-Harvest Handling and Storage

Drying: Dry MAPs to a moisture level of 10-15%, to prevent spoilage and contamination.

Storage: Store MAPs in a cool, dry, and well-ventilated area, to maintain quality and potency.

Packaging: Package MAPs in airtight containers or bags, to prevent moisture and contamination.

Labeling: Label MAPs with relevant information, such as the botanical name, date of harvest, and storage conditions.

Certification and Regulatory Compliance

Organic Certification: Obtain organic certification, such as USDA Organic or EU Organic, to ensure compliance with organic standards.

Good Agricultural Practices (GAP) Certification: Obtain GAP certification, such as GlobalGAP, to ensure compliance with GAP standards.

Regulatory Compliance: Comply with relevant regulations, such as those related to food safety, environmental protection, and labor laws.

By adopting GCAP, farmers, collectors, and producers of MAPs can ensure the quality, sustainability, and safety of their products, while also promoting environmental stewardship and social responsibility.

References

International Organizations

European Union (EU): "Council Regulation (Ec)No 834/2007 on organic production and labelling of organic products" (2007)

Food and Agriculture Organization (FAO): "The International Code of Conduct on the Distribution and Use of Pesticides" (2002)

Indian Government: "National Medicinal Plants Board (NMPb)Guidelines for Good Agricultural Practices (GAP) for Medicinal Plants" (2013)

International Organization for Standardization (ISO): "ISO 22000:2005 - Food safety management systems - Requirements for any organization in the food chain" (2005)

United States Department of Agriculture (USDA): "National Organic Program (NOP) Standards" (2010)

World Health Organization (WHO): "WHO Guidelines for Good Agricultural and Collection Practices (GACP) for Medicinal Plants" (2003)

24

Value Addition in Medicinal and Aromatic Plants

Value addition refers to the process of increasing the economic value of a product, service, or commodity through various means, such as:

Processing: Transforming raw materials into a more refined or finished product.

Enhancement: Improving the quality, appearance, or functionality of a product.

Differentiation: Creating unique features, branding, or packaging to distinguish a product from others.

Innovation: Introducing new or improved products, services, or processes.

Value addition in medicinal and aromatic plants (MAPs) is essential to enhance their economic value, quality, and marketability. Here are key reasons why value addition is necessary:

Enhanced economic value

Value addition increases the economic value of MAPs, benefiting farmers and stakeholders. Primary processing and value addition are crucial in this regard. For instance, drying, cleaning, grading, and packaging are essential steps in adding value to MAPs.

Improved quality and shelf life

Value addition helps preserve the bioactive compounds and aroma of MAPs, extending their shelf life. Techniques such as drying, extraction, and storage in airtight containers are vital in maintaining the quality of MAPs.

Increased market access and competitiveness

Value-added MAP products meet international quality standards, expanding market access and competitiveness. For example, essential oils, herbal teas, and phytopharmaceuticals are value-added products that cater to diverse markets.

Diversified product portfolio

Value addition enables the creation of diverse products from MAPs, catering to various industries such as cosmetics, pharmaceuticals, and food. Examples of value-added products include herbal cosmetics, medicinal supplements, and aromatherapy products.

Empowerment of rural communities

Value addition in MAPs provides employment opportunities and income generation for rural communities, promoting sustainable livelihoods. By engaging in value addition activities, rural communities can improve their economic well-being and contribute to the growth of the MAP sector.

Methods

Primary Processing

Primary processing refers to the initial stages of processing raw materials, including medicinal and aromatic plants (MAPs), to prepare them for further processing, storage, or marketing.

Objectives of primary processing

Cleaning: Removing impurities, dirt, or contaminants from the raw materials.

Sorting: Separating raw materials based on quality, size, shape, or color.

Grading: Classifying raw materials into different grades based on quality or characteristics.

Drying: Reducing the moisture content of raw materials to prevent spoilage or degradation.

Packaging: Storing raw materials in suitable containers or packaging materials to maintain quality and freshness.

Examples of primary processing in MAPs

- Cleaning and washing of fresh herbs
- Drying of medicinal plants to remove excess moisture
- Sorting and grading of botanicals based on quality or size
- Packaging of dried herbs or spices in airtight containers
- Extraction of essential oils from plant materials through steam distillation or solvent extraction

Primary processing is an essential step in preparing raw MAP materials for further processing, storage, or marketing, and helps to maintain their quality, safety, and efficacy.

Secondary Processing

Secondary processing refers to the transformation of raw materials or primary processed products into higher-value products through various physical, chemical, or biological processes.

Objectives of secondary processing

Transformation: Changing the physical or chemical properties of raw materials to create new products.

Enhancement: Improving the quality, appearance, or functionality of primary processed products.

Value Addition: Increasing the economic value of raw materials or primary processed products.

Examples of secondary processing in MAPs

- Extraction: Isolating bioactive compounds from plant materials using solvents, enzymes, or other methods.
- Fractionation: Separating essential oils into individual components or fractions.
- Formulation: Blending MAP extracts or essential oils with other ingredients to create products like herbal teas, supplements, or cosmetics.
- Encapsulation: Coating MAP extracts or essential oils with a protective layer to enhance stability or bioavailability.
- Manufacturing: Producing finished products like phytopharmaceuticals, herbal infusions, or aromatherapy products.

Secondary processing plays a crucial role in creating value-added products from MAPs, enhancing their marketability, and increasing their economic value.

Tertiary Processing

Tertiary processing refers to the final stages of processing, where value-added products from secondary processing are transformed into consumer-ready products or specialized formulations.

Objectives of tertiary processing

Product finishing: Finalizing the product's form, texture, and appearance.

Customization: Creating specialized formulations or products tailored to specific markets, customers, or applications.

Quality control: Ensuring the final product meets quality, safety, and regulatory standards.

Examples of tertiary processing in MAPs

Tableting or Capsulation: Converting herbal extracts or powdered botanicals into tablets or capsules.

Creams and Ointments: Blending herbal extracts or essential oils with bases to create topical products.

Flavoring and Coloring: Adding natural flavorings or colorings to herbal teas, supplements, or food products.

Packaging and Labeling: Final packaging and labeling of products for retail or distribution.

Quality assurance and testing: Conducting final quality control checks, testing, and certification.

Tertiary processing is the last step in the processing chain, where the focus is on creating consumer-ready products that meet quality, safety, and regulatory standards.

Benefits of value addition

Value addition offers numerous benefits to stakeholders in the medicinal and aromatic plants (MAPs) sector:

1. Increased revenue
    - Higher prices for value-added products
    - Expanded market opportunities
    - Improved profitability for farmers and processors
2. Improved quality and safety
    - Enhanced quality control measures
    - Reduced risk of contamination or adulteration
    - Compliance with regulatory standards
3. Diversified product portfolio
    - Creation of new products and product lines
    - Catering to diverse markets and customer needs
    - Reduced dependence on single products or markets
4. Competitive advantage
    - Differentiation from competitors
    - Unique selling propositions
    - Enhanced brand reputation and loyalty

5. Job creation and empowerment
    - Employment opportunities in processing, packaging, and marketing
    - Skill development and training for rural communities
    - Empowerment of women and marginalized groups
6. Reduced post-harvest losses
    - Efficient processing and preservation techniques
    - Reduced spoilage and waste
    - Improved shelf life and storage stability
7. Increased export opportunities
    - Compliance with international quality standards
    - Access to new markets and customers
    - Foreign exchange earnings and economic growth
8. Improved farmer livelihoods
    - Higher incomes and profitability
    - Improved access to markets and credit facilities
    - Enhanced social and economic well-being

By adopting value addition strategies, stakeholders in the MAP sector can capitalize on these benefits, enhance their competitiveness, and contribute to sustainable economic growth and development.

MCQ questions

1. What is the primary objective of value addition in medicinal and aromatic plants?
    a) To reduce production costs
    b) To increase economic value
    c) To improve quality and safety
    d) To reduce market competition
2. Which of the following is an example of primary processing in MAPs?
    a) Extraction of essential oils
    b) Cleaning and washing of fresh herbs
    c) Formulation of herbal teas
    d) Manufacturing of phytopharmaceuticals

3. What is the main purpose of secondary processing in MAPs?
   a) To transform raw materials into higher-value products
   b) To improve quality and safety
   c) To reduce production costs
   d) To increase market competition
4. Which of the following is an example of tertiary processing in MAPs?
   a) Extraction of bioactive compounds
   b) Tableting or capsulation of herbal extracts
   c) Cleaning and washing of fresh herbs
   d) Manufacturing of phytopharmaceuticals
5. What is the benefit of value addition in MAPs in terms of market access?
   a) Reduced market competition
   b) Increased market access and competitiveness
   c) Improved quality and safety
   d) Reduced production costs
6. Which of the following is a benefit of value addition in MAPs in terms of rural communities?
   a) Job creation and empowerment
   b) Improved quality and safety
   c) Increased market access and competitiveness
   d) Reduced production costs
7. What is the purpose of grading in primary processing of MAPs?
   a) To remove impurities
   b) To classify raw materials based on quality or characteristics
   c) To reduce moisture content
   d) To improve quality and safety
8. Which of the following is an example of value-added product from MAPs?
   a) Fresh herbs
   b) Dried herbs
   c) Herbal teas
   d) Phytopharmaceuticals

9. What is the benefit of value addition in MAPs in terms of product portfolio?
    a) Reduced dependence on single products or markets
    b) Improved quality and safety
    c) Increased market access and competitiveness
    d) Reduced production costs
10. Which of the following is a benefit of value addition in MAPs in terms of farmer livelihoods?
    a) Improved access to markets and credit facilities
    b) Reduced production costs
    c) Improved quality and safety
    d) Increased market competition

Short answer questions

1. Discuss the importance of value addition in medicinal and aromatic plants
2. Describe the primary processing steps involved in preparing raw MAP materials for further processing or marketing
3. Explain the objectives and examples of secondary processing in MAPs
4. Discuss the benefits of value addition in MAPs in terms of market access, competitiveness, and rural community empowerment
5. Describe the importance of quality control measures in value addition of MAPs, including examples of quality control checks and certification

Answers for MCQ

1. b) To increase economic value
2. b) Cleaning and washing of fresh herbs
3. a) To transform raw materials into higher-value products
4. b) Tableting or capsulation of herbal extracts
5. b) Increased market access and competitiveness
6. a) Job creation and empowerment
7. b) To classify raw materials based on quality or characteristics
8. d) Phytopharmaceuticals
9. a) Reduced dependence on single products or markets
10. a) Improved access to markets and credit facilities

References

Indian Council of Agricultural Research (ICAR) (2018) Value Addition in Medicinal and Aromatic Plants: A Handbook. New Delhi: ICAR.

Kumar, L., Bharadvaja, N., Singh, R. and Anand, R. (eds.) (2024) Medicinal and Aromatic Plants: Current Research Status, Value-Addition to Their Waste, and Agro-Industrial Potential (Vol II).

Rao, K.S., Haran, R.H. and Rajpoot, V.S. (2022) 'Value addition: A novel strategy for quality enhancement of medicinal and aromatic plants', Journal of Applied Research on Medicinal and Aromatic Plants, 31, p. 100415. doi: [insert doi]

Walker, C., DeMatteis, L. and Lienert, A. (eds.) (2021) Selecting value chains for sustainable food value chain development – Guidelines. Rome: FAO. doi: 10.4060/cb7623en.

World Health Organization (WHO) (2019) Good Agricultural and Collection Practices for Medicinal and Aromatic Plants. Geneva: WHO.

Index